WHEN YOU REMEMBER

Next Steps in Human Evolution

M. Jane Thomas

BALBOA.
PRESS

A DIVISION OF HAY HOUSE

ISBN: 978-1-4525-5002-2 (sc)
ISBN: 978-1-4525-5001-5 (e)

Balboa Press books may be ordered through booksellers or by contacting:

Balboa Press
A Division of Hay House
1663 Liberty Drive
Bloomington, IN 47403
www.balboapress.com
1-(877) 407-4847

Because of the dynamic nature of the Internet, any web addresses or
links contained in this book may have changed since publication and
may no longer be valid. The views expressed in this work are solely those
of the author and do not necessarily reflect the views of the publisher,
and the publisher hereby disclaims any responsibility for them.

The author of this book does not dispense medical advice or prescribe the use
of any technique as a form of treatment for physical, emotional, or medical
problems without the advice of a physician, either directly or indirectly. The
intent of the author is only to offer information of a general nature to help
you in your quest for emotional and spiritual well-being. In the event you use
any of the information in this book for yourself, which is your constitutional
right, the author and the publisher assume no responsibility for your actions.

Any people depicted in stock imagery provided by Thinkstock are models,
and such images are being used for illustrative purposes only.
Certain stock imagery © Thinkstock.

Printed in the United States of America

Balboa Press rev. date:5/8/2012

To every person who makes the effort to become more loving, compassionate, and understanding, you have my deepest gratitude. Together, we are creating a better world.

Table of Contents

Acknowledgements

Thank you to the beautiful and loving beings of the Pegasus Group, my personal guide, Jorel, my guardian angels and, of course, my own loving inner being. Special gratitude goes to Julie Tallard Johnson, my invaluable editor and writing instructor. Much love and thanks also go to my dear friends and teachers who have given me so much encouragement including Asia Voight, Mary Lelle, Mary Preuss Olson, Michaela Torcaso, Sue Langbehn, Mary Lou Bolen, Sherri Barrett, Nancy McGill, and many others.

I very much appreciate the support of my Mother, sister Pat, brothers, and my lovely step-daughters. Lastly, I thank my husband, Harry, for his love and unwavering support.

Introduction

There are those dreams that stand out as dreams of great clarity, emotion, and meaning. I had such a dream when I was twelve years old. In this dream, a tall and beautiful woman dressed in a white gown of Grecian style approached me. Her long hair blew gently in the wind as she walked. Surrounding her were companion animals who adored her. The animals included a tiger, a lion, deer, and rabbit. Deep serenity and unconditional love shone from her. My body filled with peace as she sent, from her heart to mine, a ray of complete acceptance and love. For an instant, my entire being filled with feelings of bliss and joy. Unfortunately, I was awakened and my euphoria was shattered. I was distraught and closed my eyes again, hoping to recapture the dream. I was unable to do so and the dream has never returned.

Many years later this woman came to represent my Higher Self. Yet, even when we are given such a dream—one that provides a glimpse of our Higher Self and the love that resides within—we tend to see this part of ourselves as separate and unattainable. Too often we experience this higher part of us as "just a dream." Although everyone's path is unique, all of us who seek peace, contentment, and joy inevitably find that our spiritual journey involves releasing our fear-based ego-mind and letting our loving nature—as represented by our Higher Self—emerge.

For many of us, the spiritual journey includes books, workshops and spiritual counselors. The effect of this focused intent and diligent work usually results in a slow, although worthwhile, transformation. For me the spiritual journey meant emerging from a frightened, nervous person who worried about most things to a calmer person who experiences increasing periods of complete peace. While this current state of being is much more pleasant than that of my past, my desire is to experience, on an ongoing basis, those blissful feelings of love, unshakable serenity, and absolute joy that come from a deep understanding of my oneness with all life. In other words, I want to be my Higher Self in every moment in this life.

As part of my journey to experience the peace that I know resides inside of me, I have spent time periodically writing in a journal. I would go into a light meditative state and receive loving, wise, and reassuring messages from my Higher Self. Eventually, through my meditations and journal writing, two beings made contact with me. These higher guides said they and numerous other high and loving beings had a message they wanted to share with the world. I received urgings from within and from others to channel this book you now hold in your hands.

The High Guides felt that a relatively short guidebook would provide a practical and easy means by which anyone can more easily obtain the "enlightened" state. At its core, their message is that all of us already have access to enlightenment. That part of us we call our Higher Self, our soul, or the term they use most, our "inner being," is a being of love. Enlightenment is merely bringing that loving aspect of our self into this physical experience on a continuing basis. The beauty is that this can take relatively little effort because this is not about being "good." Enlightenment is about simply being who we are, which is *a letting go of all that we are not.* Their message is an old one but begs to be told here again.

The World is Changing

These higher guides, who I call the Pegasus Group, verify what others have said about this world of contrast and duality. Throughout eons of time our world has served as a means to experience that which we *are not* (through the ego-mind that is based in fear) in order to more fully experience and know that which we *are* (beings of love). This ego-based world, you could say, is like a mother who teaches her child the difference between cold and hot through the presentation of contrast. In this case, love is more fully experienced through the contrasting expressions of fear and all of its associated emotions. Unfortunately, this exploration of self through duality and contrast has caused us to build and then destroy thousands of civilizations on this beautiful planet—our Gaia.

At this time in our spiritual and planetary evolution, the Pegasus Group says we will be exploring a different path—a path that will end the violence and suffering and bring forth our loving nature. ***Having experienced every aspect of fear available to us in this amazing world of contrast, the fear and suffering are no longer necessary.*** Our *memory* of these fear-based experiences will be sufficient. The veil of forgetfulness we have used each time we have incarnated in order to experience this world of duality can now be released.

We are all part of this next step of humanity's evolution. The old paradigm of dualism and contrast is ending. The Pegasus Group, through this book, provides guidance, meditations, and exercises that will assist in this personal and planetary shift. They help us to understand and challenge our beliefs, monitor thoughts and words, and raise our vibration, while showing us how to become *conscious* creators.

One of the most effective tools provided by the Pegasus Group is a simple method of accessing our wise inner being to gain insight into past traumas, transform relationships, change our beliefs, or simply to guide us as we make everyday decisions. Depending upon the strength of our intention and how hard we work to raise our vibration, achieving a high state of well-being can happen quite rapidly or take an extended period of time. For me and most others on this path, our vibration varies from high to low depending upon our ability to release the habits of our ego-mind. As we become more aware of these habits, we learn to shift our perceptions from those based in fear to those based in love. Over time, we find that our energy is vibrating at a higher level and we are residing more often in the natural loving state of our inner being.

The Benefits of a Loving State of Being

As you follow the exercises and meditations contained in this book and become more aware of the origin of your thoughts, beliefs, and emotions you will remember and connect with your inner being as I have. This loving state of being greatly expands your ability as a conscious creator, and brings you into the forefront of creating a new world based in love.

This new way of being is achievable. As you say yes to this shift in global consciousness, you say yes to your inner nature. The rewards for your effort are immediate and multiple. When you express the love that you are, you feel good. By releasing your fears, you tap into the creative force of the universe, which is love. As you examine and change your beliefs, you literally change that which you can achieve or create. And, through this change in your vibration (from a low density vibration limited by fear to a high vibration fueled by love) and through an understanding of how you create your experience, you become *conscious creators*. Your life reflects that greater harmony and benevolence and miracles become as natural as the stream that flows down the mountain.

Chapter 1

Wakening from the Dream of Duality

An Invitation from the Pegasus Group

We want to thank you for taking this journey and are confident that the rewards will be a more joyful self and planet!

We are the Pegasus Group, higher light beings who have come together to show you how to bring about the next evolutionary step of your being; that is, to continuously express the love that you carry within you here on this physical world. As we look at each one of you, we see the extraordinary bright light of your being. This natural radiance is currently hidden from most of you because of the choice you made long ago—the choice to experience contrast and duality. Nevertheless, this historical way of being can never change that which you are—*a being of light and love*. We welcome you on this journey to awaken from the dream of duality and forgetfulness you agreed to long ago for your own growth and sense of adventure. The time of remembering your inner light is upon you. Pain and suffering are no longer necessary tools in your journey toward enlightenment.

Exploring the Experience of Contrast

Let us begin by exploring the value of this human experience and how the seemingly unnecessary and irrational pain and suffering have been useful in your spiritual growth. Your soul, higher self, or inner being—terms we use interchangeably—knows only love, for it always understands its eternal nature and how inner being is one with Source, God, or All That Is. Like Source itself, your inner being evolves and finds joy and greater understanding through the creative process of life. Your soul or inner being directs this process and chooses what it will experience. Using the creative process on planet Earth, each soul has been able to express an infinite range and diversity of the many aspects of itself. Just look around and you get a glimpse of the variety and complexity of the life experience.

A soul can have an adventure as a male or female of various racial and cultural backgrounds. As well, the soul can experience being raised in a wide variety of geographic areas, social and economic structures, and educational levels. A soul can choose to explore music or art, become an engineer, farmer, nurse, a mother, father, a soldier, politician, or humanitarian.

Many souls choose more challenging lives through which even greater understanding can occur by living with physical or mental disabilities, encountering abusive childhoods, undergoing difficult experiences in time of war, or living in deep poverty. Throughout time, your inner being has sent a piece of itself to this planet in order to experience every possible lifestyle and every possible emotion. Since these emotions include fear-based emotions that are not an expression of inner being's loving nature, a veil of forgetfulness of your broader spiritual nature has also been an integral requirement of each Earth incarnation. You forget in order to focus on the current life you have chosen and so you will be able to completely immerse yourself in this unique world of duality.

Life on Earth is one of the most diverse experiences that a soul can have. You come into this world with the deliberate intent to forget your magnificence in order to relish the wide range of emotional experiences available to you. Feelings of hatred, resentment, jealousy, loneliness, greed, superiority, inferiority, judgment, and other such "negative" emotions are not a part of your inner being. Yet a world that provides the opportunity for you to express these emotions also provides the means for you to experience the emotions of tolerance, forgiveness, gratitude, compassion, kindness, and generosity, which are all aspects of love and a reflection of your inner being.

With this range of emotions from fear to love, you have not only set yourselves on adventures not available to your inner being, who knows only love, but through this world of contrasts, you are better able to understand the love that you are. In a way, think of living a life where you have been totally cared for and loved and have known nothing else. Without having a contrasting experience, you are not fully able to understand and appreciate the love that flows to you and is within you. You may "know" you are love, yet the full "experience" of that love is elusive. On this planet of contrasts, you can love the "unlovable." You can forgive the "unforgiveable." You can show compassion and kindness toward those in pain. You can also be the "unlovable" or the "unforgiveable" one and understand how you were brought to that place. These experiences help your inner being, who is love and is surrounded by love, to more fully understand that which *is* love.

The Wonder of Your Inner Nature

So the lives you have lived on Earth are both part of an exciting game launched by your inner being and the means by which you better understand that which you are by experiencing that which you are not. With each incarnation, your inner being gains, through experience, a better understanding and appreciation of its loving nature. Your lives on this amazing planet of contrasts are not punishment or karmic retribution. You are a beautiful, loving part of Source and Source does not punish itself. Rather, Source (and inner being) seeks to understand itself better through experience. And, as we have made clear, love cannot be fully understood without the experience of that which is not love.

You do this by studying, if you will, all aspects of love and its opposite—fear. One aspect of fear can be labeled "cruelty." Cruelty is not fully understood unless a being has been both a victim and perpetrator of cruelty. Inner being may choose a life where he will be a victim of violence after a past life of cruelty and violence to others. Some may find this distinction of balancing experience versus karma confusing, but we wish to make clear that there is not a direct and mathematical accounting of experience whereby you make a "mistake" or use bad judgment and are punished with an equally bad experience.

In the end, it is inner being's own decision to create whatever balance of experience she feels is necessary for the fullest possible understanding of that which is love. No other being or "karmic" law will make that decision for your inner being.

Each life experience, therefore, is an outcome of the inner being's desire for adventure, a means to challenge its creative abilities and, most of all, as an avenue to better know itself. Suffering, anger, and violence are called illusions since they do not affect that which you are. They have been most useful in helping you better understand and experience compassion, kindness, tolerance and other aspects of love that, in your pure state of love, are concepts less deeply understood because of the lack of contrast. At this time in your history you have sufficient memory of these contrasting emotions and are ready to play in this beautiful world with a fuller knowledge of your loving inner nature. The adventure is about to change!

Most people on the planet do not know that the game has changed and are still trapped in their fearful ego-mind. They are unaware of their union with Source and the ability each has to create with their inner being. In fact, throughout your many lives on this planet, you and your fellow beings have been so immersed in the illusory physical experience that what takes place outside of you seems to have little to do with you. Many of you have come to believe you have limited control over your life. It is as though you have stepped upon a stage and immersed yourself so thoroughly in the play, you have forgotten you are both the actor *and* director of your life. Nothing occurs in life by chance or by accident. As you open to the concept that you are the creator of your experience, you become a *conscious creator* of your life. We are here to help you *remember* that you do direct your life and that you create with others the events in your world. And, we are here to help you be fully involved in this new adventure.

The power that you hold within you is far more than most people can imagine. Your creative abilities are a reflection of the Creator or Source with whom you are an expression. Your essence (and that of everything else) is made up of the living divine consciousness of God, and that consciousness is, at its core, love. Because you are a part of Source, you not only use the universal laws of the creative process as Source does, but *you have access to Source* as you connect with your inner being. ***There are no limits to that which you can create except the limits that are self-imposed by the beliefs you hold.***

Having said this (in recognition of your unlimited abilities as spiritual beings), we acknowledge that the group mind or group belief system creates powerful limits for the vast majority of individuals. In part, this has allowed you to experience duality. In part, these common beliefs enable you to immerse yourself more completely into the physical aspects of your world. Nevertheless, as your awareness of your spiritual nature increases, you more easily overcome these shared beliefs and the "unthinkable" then becomes possible.

A Joyous Time of Awakening

The veil of forgetfulness that up until now has been useful for your inner being is thinning. You live in an extraordinary and joyous time of awakening—of remembrance. All souls who chose to incarnate at this time did so with the intention of remembering their loving nature without contrast and duality. These souls (of which you are one) realize that the experiences of suffering, lack, loss, wars, separation, and violence are no longer contributing to your spiritual evolution.

Sadly, as mentioned, many on the planet are still immersed in the illusion of fear and are unaware of their role in creating their experience and that of their world. Each being reacts differently to the density of the planet and the influence of their personal environment. They may also be balancing the experience of a past life or assisting another being in balancing their life by being the "abuser" to the other's "victimhood." Souls with greater numbers of incarnations are better able to understand their loving nature than those with many fewer incarnations. Fortunately, as more souls remember and begin to express their eternal loving nature, the world itself will begin to change and more and more will awaken out of this sleep of forgetfulness. This period of transition, in which you creatively "heal" your planet and all who inhabit it, will bring your inner being excitement and a great joy, which will last a good long time.

Remember you are, first and foremost, *creative* beings. Creating is what you love to do. You build new societies. You tear them down. You go to the moon. You come back. Life is a marvelous amusement park where your inner being goes on the scary rides and into the haunted mansions knowing they are not "real," while feeling the emotions of anticipation, uncertainty, and excitement nonetheless.

At this unique moment in history, your joy and creativity will be focused on creating new political and economic structures that bring your beloved world back into balance. The climate of war will be changed to one of peace. Above all else, this great remembering brings back into your conscious knowing the Oneness of all things and the love that is the basis of Life itself. You have set out on a new adventure as exciting and creative as those of the past only, *this time,* without the requirement of duality and contrast, you will bring into your world more of who you really are—a being of love, peace, and great joy.

Opening to the New Paradigm

To be part of this shift into a world free of dualism and conflict, you have to step outside of the ego you have so dearly identified with and become an open vessel for your inner being. Over time and with the agreement between the beings on Earth and those who watch over the Earth, the vibration of the planet has been gradually increasing. More recently, the vibration is accelerating at a more rapid pace, and the shake-ups in your economy, politics, and environment are a result of this timely shift.

For a while, those who deny the reality that all beings are one together and who are holding fast to their fear-based ego, will appear to grow stronger as they present a clear choice to the world between the illusion of fear and the truth of love. Gradually, there will be a recognition of fear for the illusion that it is, and those souls will be viewed with understanding and compassion. Once there is no longer resistance and righteous indignation toward their views, their "power" virtually fades away.

Waking Up From the Long Sleep

This paradigm shift is dependent upon a sufficient number of individuals awakening to their loving nature. Enough of you need to *remember* who you are. And who are you? You are spiritual beings having a physical experience *of your creation*. This recollection is the initial step in the process of reclaiming your spiritual and evolutionary power. As you awaken from this sleep of forgetfulness, your ego and its fears and long-held habits must be deliberately and consciously faced in order for you to see the world through loving and compassionate eyes. You must become a vigilant observer of your thoughts and beliefs. If you do this, you come to a more compassionate and objective understanding of why your life is unfolding as it is.

All of you have the potential to achieve this awakening. This requires going beyond accepting this as a possibility, to living each day in line with that which you desire to become. This effort to bring forth your loving nature is a *choice* that each of you make. Although the awakening of many creates an easier path for others to follow, there will still be those unable to shake off their fears. They will not be lost, however, for as part of Source, they will remember and rejoice when they are ready.

You are a part of this shift to a greater knowing of the creative power that lies within. And, your ability to create your desires will be magnified when you come from a place of love rather than from the fear-based ego-mind for, as you tap into your inner being, you access the loving force of the universe.

Unity with the Heart of the Universe

Connecting to the creative wellspring of the universe can be accomplished in many ways, but all ways result in achieving a higher or more loving vibration. You sense this vibration as a feeling of deep well-being or peace. This is your indicator that you are in tune with your loving inner being and, thus, with Source itself.

In obtaining a higher level of vibration, it is not necessary for you to achieve what you might call "enlightenment," or for you to completely eliminate your blockages or other aspects of your personality you deem deficient or damaged. Instead, we would say that the more often you place yourself in this higher, more peaceful space, the more quickly the fear-based ego issues that keep you from enjoying life fade away without significant effort. You naturally witness others with more compassion and less judgment. You become less obsessed with the past and no longer worry about the future. Your life flows with ease and grace. You then recognize your role as the creator of your experience, not a victim of circumstance.

Masters throughout time have provided this material in various forms. This is especially the case today as these messages are being more broadly spread through self-help books, channeled books, movies, the Internet, and TV shows. Eventually, this message will be spread most effectively one person at a time as each individual provides both an example to others and increases the world's vibration through their own efforts. Those witnessing your transformation more easily remember *their* own loving nature and, with *imagination* and *intent,* will help create a more harmonious and joy-filled world. The heart of the Universe will shine through individuals one by one, awakening everyone in their path.

Chapter 2

Merging with Your Inner Being

So how do you achieve this marvelous state of well-being as you busily go about your daily activities? Once in this state of peace, how can you use the creative ability within you? We, the Pegasus Group, offer a number of possible paths and practices to assist you in finding your own unique way toward expressing your loving inner being, creating a joy-filled life, and letting your fear-based ego fall gently away.

In this chapter, we present a basic guided meditation to use when you wish to connect directly with your inner being and enjoy its unconditional love. You can also use the meditation to simply enter a peaceful state and raise your vibration. This meditation will provide a starting place for all the meditations or exercises we offer you when accessing your inner being. In the meditation, each of you will be creating a special place of peace and high vibration that is specific to you. This is a place where you easily experience yourself as completely safe, content, and loved.

In this chapter, we also provide a guided meditation that gives you a feeling of deep calm and union with *All That Is*. Each of these meditations raises your vibration, allowing a rest from your active ego-mind while helping you merge with your loving inner being. The more often you place yourself in this higher vibration, the better you are able to release your fears and experience the bond you naturally have with all of Life.

Extending This Loving Vibration

Every moment you spend in this place of loving vibration means fewer moments spent in the lower vibration energies of fear, worry, or judgment. By training your mind to be at ease during meditation, replicating those peaceful feelings can become a way of life. When you become upset due to a personal issue or concern about the world, you will know how to retreat into meditation and bring your emotions back into a peaceful state.

As you expand the percentage of your days spent in this higher vibration energy, your life unfolds with greater ease and satisfaction. You are changing the world as you practice these meditations. Since all beings need not change their attitude and beliefs for this global shift to higher consciousness to come about, your efforts generate a significant amount of merit. Only a small percentage of the population who are vibrating at a high level are required to change the world and gift the remaining beings with these feelings of peace and love and oneness with all.

Merging with Your Inner Being – A Guided Meditation

For dedicated practitioners of meditation, the observation and letting go of all thought can bring one to that peaceful place of presence that lies between thoughts until "no thought" is the result. Sometimes, a focus on a word, phrase, or mantra can assist in this process. For many, achieving this state of well-being is made easier through a guided meditation that allows an individual's mind to focus on a scene or situation in order to create a sense of peace. This is what this meditation is designed to achieve. What we wish you to know is that this state of " well-being" can be achieved relatively easily with a simple change in focus. Further, once you become somewhat practiced, you will no longer require extended periods of alone time, although you may find that you enjoy these times of periodic refreshment.

Step 1: Setting the Stage

Allow yourself fifteen to thirty minutes of uninterrupted time in a place that is comfortable and quiet and where you are unlikely to be disturbed. When you are sitting comfortably, close your eyes and focus on your breathing. With each breath, allow your body to relax on each out breath. Notice any areas of the body that are tense and breathe into them, releasing their tension until you are completely relaxed.

Step 2: Stating an Intention

Either aloud or in silence, state your intention to merge with your inner being and achieve a state of peace and well-being.

Step 3: Creating Your Special Place

Let your imagination take you to a place you associate with serenity and relaxation. This will be your unique place—a place you have been to or a place you conceive. Your special place will come to you naturally as you allow your imagination to relax and open. You may try out several places and, in fact, your special place may change from time to time. Your place could be the shore of a beautiful lake or the ocean, under a great elder tree, in a meadow of wildflowers, or a special cabin in the woods. You could even find yourself in a cathedral or a chapel with which you have a strong association.

Some of you may see this vision clearly when you close your eyes. Or, you may experience an inner knowing, whereby you simply have a sense of what is before you—what your place looks like in all its characteristics—without actually seeing a clear picture. You may also hear words that talk of your special place, or get a direct feeling. You may have a sense of the wind, the warmth of the sun, the coolness under the trees, or smell the salt air or the moist earth. These experiences are all the ways in which your inner being holds a conversation with you. As you progress in your meditation practice you become more familiar with the language of your inner being.

In all cases, you know you are in a conversation with your inner being because you are in a peace-filled or joyful state. Even when you are dealing with such emotions as grief or sadness you still feel a deep love and acceptance. Should you experience fear or judgment, you know your ego-mind has intervened. If this happens, simply thank your ego for its concern and ask it lovingly to step aside so you may communicate with your inner being, and then continue. Your intention to connect with your inner being and, if you are having difficulty, your request for assistance from your spirit guides or angelic companions, will help you in this exercise.

When you have arrived at your special place, take time to experience it fully. Look around you. What colors do you see or sense when you look at the field of flowers, the lake or ocean, the stone of the cottage, or the clouds in the sky? What types of trees are dominant? Are there any animals, birds, or insects residing there? Do you recognize any of them? Is the weather cool or warm? Is the air still or is there a breeze? What are you wearing? Can you smell the flowers, the salt air, or the moist earth? What emotions are you experiencing in your special place? Are you excited? Do you recognize your special place? Are you happy or peaceful?

Step 4: Asking Your Inner Being to Appear

Once you have become familiar with your special place and are now relaxed, ask your inner being to appear before you. Your inner being may either stand in front of you or sit in a chair opposite you. Trust what you see or experience. Your inner being may appear as a man, woman, as an angelic being, or simply as a being of light. It could even take the form of a wizened old woman, an animal, a Native American, or a jester. If you do not see or sense your inner being, just know he or she is there. Again, your intention and desire will bring about this encounter. Give yourself permission to imagine your inner being. What do you imagine he or she looks like?

As you face your inner being, look into his or her eyes and relish the great love that is there for you. Spend time absorbing this unconditional love. Imagine this love washing over you and taking away any cares that you may have. Should tears begin to flow, let them flow. If smiles, laughter or feelings of joy come up, let them. Reside in this beautiful place for as long as you wish.

Step 5: Gratitude and Returning

When you have received as much of this love as you desire for this session, thank your inner being and tell him or her you will return another time. Slowly open your eyes, and bring yourself back into your room. Spend a little time relishing this feeling of well-being. Remember this feeling and see if you can return to it throughout the day.

This is the foundational instruction for many of the other meditations and exercises in this book. As you continue communing with your inner being we show you how you can receive compassionate and wise guidance, personal healing, and conscious creation of your experience and even that of your world.

A Meditation to Experience Peace and Oneness with the Universe

For people who meditate on a regular basis, in addition to being pleasantly relaxed and peaceful, there is the benefit of feeling a part of Source or All That Is. This consciousness raises your vibration and brings you closer to that which your inner being experiences always. Your inner being knows that she is part of the One and, thus, not separate from everything and everyone that makes up all of life. The following guided meditation is one of many that can assist in bringing about this feeling. Use this meditation when you wish to relax deeply, merge with the universe, and better understand your inner being.

Step 1: Setting the Stage

Find a quiet place where you will not be disturbed for twenty or thirty minutes and enter a relaxed state. If you wish, call in your inner being, guides, angels, and any ascended masters with whom you have a close association, to assist you in the meditation.

Step 2: Leaving the Body

Imagine yourself leaving your body and, with your spirit body, flying out beyond the planets in our solar system into the next solar system. Keep moving outward until you are in deep, dark space.

Step 3: Arriving in Deep, Dark Space

When you have reached this space, consider that the darkness is not completely black – it is closer to purple black. The dark is "the womb that gives birth to the light."

As you enter this space, you find yourself floating. Imagine the dark light penetrating your body, your muscles, your skin, and all of your organs. Sense how this purple black light is a different kind of light. The dark is still a part of the universal light.

Step 4: Experiencing Oneness with the Universe

Now experience a deepening unity with the universe and all the sensations that go along with it. When you can go no deeper, try going deeper again until you become one with the universe. You may almost disappear. Experience the complete oneness and unity as if the start of you and the deep light edges are blurred. Enjoy this space for as long as you like. Open yourself to any messages, emotions, or visual experiences you may receive from the light.

Step 5: Returning to Your Body and Recording Your Experience

After you have enjoyed the oneness and received whatever message you might have asked for, return once again to your quiet space on planet Earth and record your experience.

Chapter 3

The World of Vibration

In this chapter we discuss the world of vibration and how you and all consciousness, whether animate or inanimate, are made up of vibration. Everything in the universe is subject to movement, whether you can see it or not. You, and all that is, are elements of light and sound that vibrate, each to your own *energy signature.* This vibration and the personal energy signature discussed later in this chapter varies from high to low and blends with and influences its surroundings. Your individual vibration, therefore, has impact—some of which you can readily see and most of which you cannot.

You are reminded of how your thoughts and words create vibration and how small efforts to raise your vibration can make a significant difference in the lives of others. As well, you understand how each person contributes to the vibration of the world, thus influencing and creating major world events such as wars, efforts toward peace, economic climates, social movements, and even major weather-related occurrences. We will provide simple examples of how you can use or manipulate your environment to keep your personal vibration at a higher and more enjoyable level.

All of these concepts, of course, you know intuitively. Our hope is to have these gentle reminders brought to the forefront of your mind. You then become ever more aware of your current state of vibration. Further, you understand how your vibration affects others and your world, and how you can consciously shape your vibration to bring it more in line with your loving inner being.

Setting the Tone of Your Life

When you merge with your inner being, you vibrate at an exceptionally high vibrational level. This means you have achieved a strong and clear bond with Source. *At a higher level of vibration you attract events and people who are also vibrating at that frequency.* Most likely you still encounter negative experiences, for you may have other reasons for bringing them about. You will, however, handle such circumstances with increased grace and kindness.

As a powerful spiritual being connected with the love that is Source, your thoughts, words, feelings, and actions impact and change your world. You do not have to acknowledge this, for you are a part of the vibration that makes up the *world's* vibration. However, you can *intentionally influence* the world's vibration. If you wish to see greater peace in the world, then *be at peace.* Your vibrations of tolerance, understanding, and compassion create more of the same. Your actions of love to the Earth and all species that reside on her help others open their hearts. Be what you wish the world to be. Even so, do not resist what you do not want to see through denial or judgment. You will be as the stone dropped in the water, changing the vibration of the world in ever widening circles.

Contributing to a Better World One Smile at a Time

Even in the seemingly small events in your life your higher vibration has a significant and lasting impact. When it comes to saving the world, small actions count. Each of you has had the experience of your mood changing for the better when encountering someone who exudes happiness and good humor. Conversely, you have had your mood plummet when exposed to a person who is sad, angry, or irritable. These are seemingly small encounters with a big impact. People convey a range of vibration, from high to low, and these vibrations intersect and affect one another.

Consider further your impact on family, friends, pets, acquaintances, and strangers when you smile, provide sincere compliments, or do small kindnesses. When you are peaceful and others are stressed, your mellow state of being can help them slow down and see things in a more positive light. Each individual act, no matter how small, makes a difference. And, through your connectedness, such expressions of love and well-being have a cascading affect far beyond the one kind word or smile.

The Cascading Effect of Kindness

Your kindness at work, for example, can make your colleague's drive home more pleasant. He or she arrives home in a happier state of mind and their spouse responds in kind. The natural exuberance of the children is more easily tolerated and interactions are more harmonious. The father may take the time to play soccer with his daughter or build a model plane with his son. The mother may tell the children a story from her past, give them a cooking lesson as she makes dinner, or read them a favorite tale. The children could see a special moment of affection between the mother and father. That one night of good will could stick in a child's memory for the rest of her life and give the child a new direction and improved self-worth. You may never witness the effect of your smile, sense of peace, or kindnesses shared, yet its impact is far wider than you imagine.

The Vibrational Signature of Words

You can see how your kind words, understanding smile, and a freely given helping hand generate a high vibration and positive influence. Because they are so important, however, we wish to briefly touch on how your thoughts and words may be more powerful than you currently view them. First, remember you are the "director" of your life. That which you believe firmly, feel strongly, and express through your intention, thoughts, and words, are the means by which you direct and create your experience. We will talk more about this important concept in later chapters.

The other aspect of your words (and the intentions and emotions behind them) that deserves attention is the vibration they create. Your emotional state (uplifted or discouraged, guilty or light-hearted, resentful or understanding) will tell you whether the vibration you create is higher (more loving) or lower (fear-based). You can actually feel these words in your body and this vibration acts as a magnate to draw to you people and events of a similar vibration.

If you desire to keep your energy signature high, it makes sense to observe and modify your words and the intention and emotion behind those words. Notice what you say and how those words affect the body. Perhaps your stomach is queasy or your shoulders tighten or your head begins to ache. If the words you speak have you feeling badly, make a conscious choice not to repeat those words.

Every moment is a moment of choice and you can decide to speak with greater patience, kindness, and understanding. Over time, your habits will change to the benefit of your energy signature. Take the time now to create a new intention—*"My intention is to think and speak in a way that is kind, loving, compassionate, and understanding to all people and beings in my life."* Do your very best in each moment to honor that intention without getting too discouraged over your progress.

Words are tied up with your beliefs and how you handle past traumas and current life experiences. Therefore, as you continue your path toward expressing the highest part of you, observe and monitor your words. This helps you determine how well you are doing and provides insights into that which is keeping you from your peaceful and loving center. In this book we offer many suggestions and exercises to aid you in becoming more aware of your words so that you may modify them as necessary. Use these tools freely, as well as the numerous other books and teachers to whom you are drawn. As challenging as this process may seem, the happy result is a more loving vibration.

Participating in the Group Mind

More difficult to see is the role each individual plays in creating world events. While those who rule by fear appear to have the greatest impact on society, what you are observing is the dominant reflection of the group mind.

Dictators, certain corporate leaders, members of the media who focus on negative events, murderers and terrorists, and even certain religious leaders are merely reflections of many minds immersed in fear. The fear-based ego-mind is concerned with survival and believes you are separate from all others. The ego-mind also believes there is not enough for all to survive or prosper.

According to the ego-mind, the world is a frightening place. The ego seeks to protect you by holding on to strong beliefs where people are separate and beliefs are divided into camps of either "good" or "bad." To protect these personal beliefs, the ego-mind must be "right," making others "wrong." This leads to states of being that are immersed in judgment, superiority, anger, righteousness, irritability, cruelty, and the assertion of will over others. On the other side of the equation, are the more passive states of guilt, depression, lack of self-worth, and feelings of powerlessness. These states of being are of a low vibration. They are not accurate reflections of your inner being, which is love. Nevertheless, they are a means of creation.

Each individual lost in the fearful ego-mind has relatively little power. However, when they are joined with others immersed in fear, violence and destruction result. This can take the form of natural disasters, political outcomes, financial meltdowns, or other major events. For thousands of your earth years, the dominant thought patterns based in fear and separation have created the endless wars, violence, bigotry, poverty, disease, subjugation, and even murder or enslavement of entire populations. As individuals, you create and draw to you the experiences of your life. With others, you create the broader events of your society and world.

Keeping Hold of the Stronger Vibration of Love

Fortunately, the fear-based ego-mind is not the stronger means of creation, nor does it encompass or influence others as widely as does an individual who resides in her peaceful center or inner being. Love is real. Fear is the illusion you have created in order to experience duality. While many can be cowed by their fearful thoughts, one individual standing in truth and compassion can move many to positive action. Ghandi and Martin Luther King are two such examples of this principle.

As you spend increasing time in the space of love and peace, you discover that people are naturally drawn to you. Further, you help them raise their vibration for, in you, they recognize their own loving nature. This may not be a conscious recollection, yet they find their spirits are lifted, they think more clearly, and receive insights into ways they can improve their own vibration and, thus, their own happiness. *The more time you can hold onto this higher vibration, the greater your sphere of influence.*

Siddhartha Guatama (the Buddha), Jesus the Christ, Mohammed, Ghandi, Paramahansa Yogananda, Sri Eknath Eswaran, Mother Teresa, and many others exemplified this expanded positive influence. The Dahlai Lama is an example of a current master who, with only his presence, influences positively those who are near him, those who follow him from afar, and even those who do not know him or know *of* him. Indeed, we all hold this ability to cast our influence far beyond our immediate circles. As shown above, you need not be at the level of a Buddha or Christ to expand your positive influence throughout the world. A simple smile will do. *Focus on each moment and what you can do to influence the vibration of this moment.*

These instances of peace and love add up and are part of a continuum allowing you to re-member with your inner being. From birth, you create habits and beliefs that act like grooves in a record. Once set, you require effort to make new grooves or habits. Awareness and intention to establish new habits will change a life anchored primarily in fear to one that is anchored in love. The idea here is to make love your habitual response to all that you encounter. You do this by raising your energy signature.

Energy Signatures

The vibration that each of you send out is your ***energy signature***, which reflects the degree of love or fear in which you currently reside. On the other side of that are the vibrations emanating from all that surround you, for all things are part of the one consciousness and have their own energy signature. You can use other elements in your environment to elevate your energy in a more loving and peaceful direction. Many of these elements you gravitate toward naturally. Nevertheless, a greater awareness of how you are affected by your vibratory environment will help you more often seek ways to support a higher energy signature. Like the practice of meditation, in which you consciously seek to deepen your sense of peace, you can manipulate or use your environment to similarly affect your feeling of well-being.

All things are made up of vibration. You are, in fact, surrounded by a sea of energy. As you become aware of this, you can begin to evaluate each being and your surroundings in light of whether you feel better or worse when you encounter them. This can range from the energy signature of your cat or dog, to a walk through the woods, to the energetic quality of a party, or a ride on a bus, or a trip to a beautiful cathedral. Although you cannot always avoid situations where the energy signature is obviously uncomfortable or low, you can learn to stay in your peaceful center regardless of what is happening around you. Until such time as this becomes the norm for you, seek out those aspects of your environment that have a higher energy signature and use that to raise your own vibration.

Let's now review a few examples of ways to use your environment for this purpose and let this trigger your own ideas for tapping into this amazing sea of energy.

Creating a Higher Energy Signature within the Home and at Work

Music is an obvious physical demonstration of an energy signature. Certain types of music are soothing to the body, while others evoke joy or heightened energy. There is music that will aggravate the body, as will loud and repetitive noises over a contracted period of time. Singing with joy and enthusiasm has a positive affect on the overall physical body. For many individuals, music can be one of the quickest means of releasing anger, depression, lack of energy, and feelings of unease. We recommend that you use music in your life to elicit peace or joy when needed, as well as when you find your energy getting low.

Everything you do to support the well-being of your body brings a higher vibration to your physical body. When you hurriedly eat a meal of little nutritional value with only passing thought to its taste, you are not bringing in the optimum level of vibration to fuel your body. Instead, take time to experience your food. Enjoy its preparation; admire its inherent beauty and the wonder of how your food is grown. Enjoy the delicious scents as you cook your meal and notice how the combination of ingredients enhances the flavor of the food. Present your feast in a way that maximizes its beauty and eat your food in gratitude for its gift of life. When you eat in this way, you improve the energy signature of the meal itself and absorb the highest vibration the food has to offer.

The energy signature of your home influences your well-being even as you sleep. A home that is clean and free of clutter is more restful to the mind. Organization of often-used items, such as keys, clothes, and tools, can save time and minimize stress when they are easily and quickly located. Further, when furniture, plants, and decorative items are in good condition and arranged with an eye toward beauty, feelings of satisfaction and well-being are promoted. The positive energy signature of the home is increased when you create beauty and harmony and bring to your home a sense of peace and serenity rather than aggravation and disorder.

These same principles of enhancing the energy signature of your home can be applied to your work environment. For many of you, a large percentage of time is spent in an office. Like your home, create a strong and vibrant energy signature by keeping your office organized and clean. In a more uplifted environment your enjoyment and efficiency increases. When you are more content, your fellow workers benefit and, consequently, their own energy signatures are enhanced. Your feelings of peace and satisfaction carry over as you drive home and as you interact with your family, especially when you choose to improve your driving energy signature.

The Energy Signature of the Natural World

The natural world is a very good place to absorb a high vibration. Source consciousness is in all things and one of the purest, most accessible states is to be found in the natural environment because the natural world is not caught up in the ego-mind.

Regardless of your current circumstances, you experience wealth beyond measure when you do as you were meant to do—explore the sheer physical beauty of this world. When you spend time in nature, you are brought into the present moment, your body is more active, and your mind is less engaged in the ego. If you are watching the antics of baby foxes at play, you are fully engaged in the present moment. Interacting with the natural world usually requires walking and the use of your eyes, ears, and sense of touch and smell. By focusing on the present moment and a full engagement of the body and its senses, the ego-mind is quieted. Then the joy of interacting with the physical world awakens deep feelings of harmony, exhilaration, and contentment in you. Nature seeps into your being and you recognize yourself in it for—after all—you are part of the natural world.

You can enhance your experience in nature by engaging all of your senses. Can you smell the earth that has just been turned over in the field? Is that the scent of rain about to fall? Do you smell the salt of the ocean or the pine in the forest? How pleasant is the breeze as it gently moves about your face and hair? Is the sun warming your skin or is the cold seeping through your jacket? Do you hear the birds calling to each other and the rustle of grasses in the wind? How beautiful are the colors in the water, trees, and grasses?

Have you ever noticed how these colors always blend and are never harsh?

Finally, just sit with the water or the rock or the tree and let your consciousness merge with it. What is your sense of time when you merge with the rock or the mountain? What would that rabbit tell you if you opened to its view of life? Can you imagine what the water would show you if you followed the stream on its journey through the town, into the country, and beyond to the ocean?

Time spent immersed fully in nature brings you a sense of peace, gratitude, and joy in life. Again, the more often you place yourself within a higher vibration state, such as that found in the natural world, the easier it will be to recognize and release the emotions of the ego-mind and reside in your more natural state of love.

A Meditation: Merging with Mother Earth

The following meditation allows you to experience the consciousness of a rock, how the rock uses energy, and how the rock relates to the passage of time. Use this meditation as a means of accessing the wisdom of the rock and Mother Earth.

Step 1: Setting the Stage

Give yourself fifteen to thirty minutes for this meditation. Find a quiet space where you will not be disturbed. Ground yourself into Mother Earth. You can do this by imagining that your legs are intertwined with the roots of a tree that go deep into the

Earth. Or you can simply imagine yourself sitting with your back against a large oak tree. You should now feel centered, calm, and grounded with the Earth. Relax and breathe with the tree.

Step 2: Finding and Communing with the Rock

Now imagine yourself entering a large cave where there is a small amount of light that guides you to a beautiful rock. Notice what your cave looks and feels like and, as you do, find a large rock that calls to you. The rock could be sitting on the ground before you or contained in the wall. Sit down in your cave and focus your attention on this rock. After a few moments ask permission to merge with the rock.

When you have received permission, become one with your rock by letting your consciousness merge with the sensations, the perspective, and the wisdom within the rock. Let yourself settle into sharing the energy signature of the rock. In turn, let the rock tell you of its purpose on earth. Then ask the rock about your purpose in life and request guidance to help you in achieving this purpose.

Step 3: Returning to Your Room and Recording Your Experience

When you have spent sufficient time with the rock, send your gratitude for its time and wisdom. Then slowly bring yourself back into your room and record all that you received during this merging meditation.

Chapter 4

Increasing Your Energy Signature

You are now ready to increase your energy signature with practices found in this chapter—practices designed to use in your daily life. As you make the effort to change your perceptions and habitual way of doing things, remind yourself often that it is in your nature to vibrate at your highest and most beautiful frequency. Each time you succeed makes the next time easier.

An Exercise – Transforming Daily Difficulties

Achieving a state of peace and joy in life happens with a shift in perception. Let us imagine, for the moment, that you are stuck in traffic and are late for an appointment. Or, you might be at the airport awaiting your luggage or standing in the "wrong" line at the grocery store. Perhaps you are in a staff meeting at work and the atmosphere is tense. In these circumstances, the ego-mind has a tendency to get impatient and irritated and sees others and outside circumstances as impeding its progress. The ego-mind does not want to take responsibility for transforming these negative situations. The feelings of anger or resentment begin to expand and soon you can be fuming over circumstances that are "out of your control."

Initially, your efforts to transform irritation, impatience, or anger into something more pleasant can be daunting. However, if you can view these difficulties as opportunities to practice bringing forth your higher nature, you can make these exercises a challenging game that benefits you and others in many ways. Here is how:

Begin by reminding yourself that **vibration attracts** *circumstances to you. Do this with compassion. Understand that the external circumstances are, in some way, mirroring an inner belief or condition. To gain insight into the reasons you have drawn this particular circumstance to you or to put it all into a higher perspective, relax and move into the mode of the "Silent Observer."*

The Silent Observer is a place of witnessing what is arising in the present moment without getting caught up in the emotionality or judgment of it. There is no drama, for you are merely observing life as it occurs. Your senses become more acute as you allow yourself to bring attention to your surroundings. You can do this by incorporating all the different senses in your observations. As part of this process, don't forget to include witnessing your emotional responses to the situation.

Step 1: Setting the Stage

In order to prepare yourself to become the Silent Observer, you need to completely relax. A reliable method of relaxation is to become aware of the state of your body and address any areas of tension. Start with several deep breaths, and with every out breath experience a further relaxation of your body. Let your thoughts drift away until you notice you are simply observing what you are seeing without commentary or judgment.

Step 2: Expanding Your Aura

After this period of observation and relaxation, take a moment to ask your inner being to come to the forefront. Perhaps you gain clarity as to the cause of this traffic blockage or other difficulty. Perhaps the reason no longer matters. Either way, let a sense of peace well up inside of you as your inner being surfaces. Use your imagination to see the aura of your being expand so that this aura covers your entire body, going out from your body several feet. See your loving aura expand further, encompassing the people adjacent to you. Continue in this expansion until the entire traffic jam, meeting, or line of people, are surrounded by your aura of love. Then reside in this beautiful place and know that all is well. See all involved through the eyes of your inner being, sense your connection with them, and witness their core being that is love.

This exercise provides a diversion from the more habitual response and places you in a higher level of vibration, increasing your energy signature. Difficulties such as these present you with opportunities to either perpetuate a lower vibration or increase to a higher vibration. Since you cannot express both vibrations simultaneously, inherent in each difficulty lies the jewel of energetic transformation. A further benefit of this practice may be a quicker resolution to whatever problem or circumstance you encounter and you soon find yourself with a great feeling upon which to base the remainder of your day.

Elevating the Energy Signature of Your Relationships

Naturally, you want to raise the vibration of your relationships. Like most people, you probably notice a repetition of old patterns of interaction without knowing how to break them. These patterns of conflict could be with people you encounter every day, such as loved ones, friends, or work colleagues. Uncomfortable patterns of behavior with people you encounter only occasionally also may arise, such as the store clerk, landlord, or the phone company representative. It is easy to assume that *"if only the other person would change, our relationship would be better."* Fortunately, we are here to assure you that it only takes one to change a pattern in any relationship.

As a start, recall that your energy signature influences your interactions. If you are angry, critical, or inpatient, you draw people and circumstances to you that match or feed into this energy signature. If you are peaceful or light-hearted, this energy signature blends with and helps sooth the energy signature of others. Although people may not know what you are thinking, your thoughts, assumptions, and emotions are communicated to the other whether or not words are exchanged. This is the reason your energy signature is so influential, for it is made up of your current state of being, and it is this state of being that the other senses.

We also suggest you view all who come into your life as benevolent teachers who are illustrating different aspects of yourself that require healing or greater personal growth. Any person or circumstance that draws you away from your peaceful center is an opportunity to examine the fear that lies behind this uncomfortable emotion. Is there a fear that someone will think badly of you? Are you afraid of losing someone close to you? Are you worried about money or your livelihood? Are your beliefs being questioned or threatened?

These are a few common fears that may be triggering your uncomfortable reactions to others. When you become aware of these fears, you create the opportunity to heal this wounded part of yourself or to leave that fear behind for good. Although overcoming these fears may require a variety of healing modalities over a period of time, eventually you no longer react to similar situations. Even better, these uncomfortable situations no longer occur in your life.

You will know you are raising your energy signature closer to that of your inner being when you see the people in your life and in the broader world as part of the One and connected with you. Whatever issues they have, whether hatred or intolerance, addictions, or even extreme behavior, such as violence, you see the divine that resides within each of them. If you accept their current level of consciousness, you increase your energy signature and send forth that higher vibration into the world. Equally important, you no longer give your creative energy to that which you do not want, thus benefiting both your life and that of the world.

Observation of Patterns in Relationships

To improve your relationships, *observe patterns that result in conflict.* Are there situations in which you and your spouse or you and your child invariably argue, even repeating phrases verbatim? As an example, perhaps each month you and your spouse argue over finances. Be mindful if the words you use are blaming, such as "irresponsible, spendthrift, skinflint, passive-aggressive, controlling." Are these words part of the familiar pattern? Does each person bring up the past to reinforce his position?

In such arguments each person can become defensive and focus on why they are "right" and the other person "wrong." Admitting the possibility that there might have been a better way of addressing the financial situation becomes difficult to do. Over time, patterns only get stronger each time they are repeated. You either strengthen the ego-defenses and habitual patterns or weaken them through transformational practices. When communication comes from the ego, the vibration leads to a downward spiral of resentment and recrimination as the argument is often replayed over and over in one's mind.

To release yourself from these destructive patterns, *look into the ego-mind.* While its view of life is distorted, the ego-mind is doing its best to protect you from life as it knows it. How might this be true in your case? An excellent method of gaining insight into the fears that may be fueling your argument or uncomfortable situation is to access the wisdom of your inner being. By doing so, you gain perspective regarding the underlying reasons you and your spouse, child, or friend keep repeating this pattern and how best to release this pattern of behavior once and for all. Understanding the background and circumstances that cause each person to react as they do has an immensely healing effect and allows you to view the situation with love. You then do what is best for you and all parties involved.

Your strong intention to improve your relationships and your life opens the way to lasting transformation. The transformational exercise that follows accesses your inner being and provides a sure method for understanding and change.

Writing a Letter to Your Inner Being – A Transformation Exercise

Step 1: Setting the Stage

This journal exercise can take forty-five to sixty minutes or more. If you prefer and it works better for you, divide the exercise. You can take a break after you have written your letter to your inner being and return to your inner being's response when you are ready. In either case, bring your journal with you and find a quiet and relaxing space where you will not be disturbed.

When you are comfortable, close your eyes and take several deep breaths until you are in a relaxed state.

Step 2: Going to Your Special Place

When you are completely relaxed, engage your imagination and go to the special place you created in chapter 2 ("Merging with Your Inner Being – A Guided Meditation"). Imagine your inner being coming to greet you with great joy and love for you.

After you have enjoyed a short period of time together, tell your inner being that you have a problem and would like to access his or her wisdom. Express your desire to write a letter to your inner being that will fully articulate the problem or issue. Imagine or sense your inner being telling you that she is so happy you have come to her for help. She will listen carefully to all you have to say and gladly give you her insights and advice. It does not matter if you cannot see or sense your inner being, just trust she or he is there for, in fact, you and your inner being are one.

Step 3: Corresponding with Your Inner Being

Once you have finished with Step 2 and are feeling relaxed, open your eyes and take out your journal. Begin writing a letter to your inner being describing the situation in as much detail as possible. Describe the interaction you had with the other person, how you felt, how they responded to you, how you responded to them, the way in which this interaction is similar to those you have had in the past, and anything else you deem relevant. Know that your inner being is listening with love and compassion.

Step 4: Asking Your Inner Being for Its Wisdom

After you have fully expressed yourself in your letter, requesting guidance, ask your inner being for insight into why you have drawn this argument or situation to you. Start this part of the exercise by having your inner being begin to write a letter back to you. It can begin this way—"Dearest Beloved!" Let whatever comes to your mind flow on to the paper without questioning your words until such point that you feel everything has been said.

You may also receive a visual picture, a feeling, a simple knowing, an insight, or any combination of the above. Write down any response you receive. If your response is loving and non-judgmental and feels right, you know the response is from your inner being. If the response is harsh and you feel badly or belittled, the response is from the ego-mind and you can do this exercise again at another time. If you are unable to get any response, know you will receive one later through an inspired thought, a passage in a book, the observation of a friend, or any number of other ways your inner being uses to communicate with you.

Awareness As the Key to Transformation

This time with your inner being gives you insights into reasons you are drawing these people and interactions to you. You then come to understand your part in the dynamic. You do not have to overcome the causes and conditions behind the interaction, whether these are feelings of unworthiness, perfectionism, or low self-esteem related to you or your spouse. ***Awareness alone is key to transforming your negative encounters to positive ones.*** You need only be aware of how any negative thought pattern brings about such experiences. In response, your life will mirror your new thoughts and awareness and your inner being will be brought into the forefront of your thoughts, your life, and your relationships.

Changing the Patterns "On the Spot" Using the Transformation Exercise

Exploring a recurring argument through the journaling process with your inner being allows you to understand what is occurring at a time of your own choosing, without the pressure and presence of the other individual, and within a safe environment. More challenging is to use this newfound knowledge and the transformation process while in the midst of one of these discussions. With practice you will become more skilled in doing so.

The next time you draw to you one of these unpleasant interactions, breathe deeply and slip into the role of the Silent Observer. Observe from this outside vantage point your words and feelings as well as those of the other person. As you become more aware of what you are saying and the reasons and feelings behind your words, you begin to provide a more honest, objective, and less emotion-laden response.

This is not to say you will not express what you are feeling. Instead, you express yourself in a way that does not make the other person "wrong," thus putting them in a defensive and, often, aggressive posture. When in the mode of the Silent Observer, you defuse the whole situation and allow both of you to come to a mutually acceptable solution. At the very least you agree you are both entitled to different viewpoints. You know you have succeeded when your emotional state is upbeat, you are satisfied with the outcome, and the vibration in the room is positive.

When the atmosphere is calm, invite your inner being to come into your body so that you can view the other person through the eyes of love. As with the example of the traffic jam, bring up the love of your inner being until your aura goes beyond the body. As your aura expands even more, invite the other person's inner being to merge with your aura and notice the increase in love coming to and flowing from you. Imagine the beauty of their inner being and their inner being's compassion and understanding for you as well as for their physical self. Forgive yourself and the other for any pain that resulted from your current or past interactions. Ask your inner being to bring healing to the relationship and help you see the other's inner being whenever you interact.

Over time, you may find the relationship is healed and goes on in a higher, more loving fashion. Another outcome may be that the person is no longer a part of your life. Since like attracts like, your higher vibration brings to you people of a similar vibration, and these relationships more closely reflect your aura of peace, love, and joy.

There are many situations in your life where you can use these simple steps, thus accessing your inner being for your benefit and that of others. You can practice these methods if you are in a long and time-consuming line at the bank, as you negotiate a loan, or when talking with the cable people. Every day you engage in relationships with other people and the world at large. Bringing your inner being into your conscious awareness results in a personal sense of peace and well-being and helps change the events of your life in ways you find more desirable.

Upon Awakening – Setting the Tone for Your Day

This exercise reminds you of who you are and helps to transform your days. *Each day after you awake, we suggest you take five minutes to set the tone of your day. First, state your intention to be aware of your inner loving nature as much as possible during the day. If you wish, ask for help in remembering this intention.* You can ask your inner being, your spirit guides, guardian angels, and any other beloved spirit masters you are close to such as Jesus, St. Francis, Mother Mary, and Kuan Yin. Again, remembering that all beings and all things are part of the One, know that you are never alone and help is available to you from many sources, including the spiritual realm. These higher beings would never interfere with your free will. Nevertheless, when you ask, they are always ready and willing to assist in your spiritual growth and in bringing more love and joy into your life.

After you have set your intention, spend a few moments picturing how your day is likely to unfold. See yourself getting ready for work, enjoying your breakfast, helping your spouse and children, driving to work with ease, being productive and enjoying your work, coming home, preparing dinner, enjoying time with the family and your pets, spending time with yourself or your spouse, and getting ready for a pleasant night's sleep. See everything happening with ease and satisfaction. All problems that arise are quickly solved. Relationships are enjoyable. After imagining your day, bring up your inner being and the love that is the expression of your inner being.

Expand this feeling until the aura of your inner being encompasses all of your physical body and enjoy this vibration. Then ask your inner being to expand and encompass all aspects of your day. This aura acts as a bubble of love when you are with your loved ones at home, when you are driving your car, or when you are interacting at work. Then thank your inner being for expressing itself through you throughout your day. Bring the loving vibration of your morning meditation with you as you experience each aspect of the day.

Upon Retiring – Reviewing Your Day

Before you go to sleep that night, go over your day. Remember those aspects of your day when you felt the peace and love of your inner being. Notice the times when you fell out of this pattern of peace. Ask your inner being to give you insight into the reason peace eluded you during those times and what you can do in the future to create a better outcome. If you found yourself seriously out of balance, take the opportunity, either that night or at another time, to use your journal exercise to access your inner being and obtain greater understanding.

Each time you gain insight into your actions and the reasons behind them, you better understand how to avoid such future situations. You catch yourself earlier in the process and learn how to remain in your peaceful center regardless of external circumstances. Over time, you find you no longer have these experiences and life flows with greater ease and joy.

Using Guided Meditation to Increase Your Energy Signature

Meditation of all kinds results in relaxation, the reduction of stress, and a feeling of balance. In the meditation below, you use your imagination to go to the "Center of the Light" where all life emanates and bring back an increased percentage of higher vibration (in the form of light) into your being.

Step 1: Setting the Stage

Go to a quiet, comfortable space where you will not be disturbed for twenty or thirty minutes. Breathe deeply. Then use a progressive relaxation technique by starting at your head, neck, and shoulders, and working your way down, relaxing each part of your body until your body is completely relaxed. Call on your guides and angels for their assistance.

Step 2: Traveling to the Center of the Light

Now imagine separating your spirit body from your physical body and ask your spirit body to be taken to the "Center of the Light" where all life emanates throughout the universe.

Experience yourself as joy, light, bliss, release, expansion, and understanding. Immerse yourself in this huge space of light from which all life emanates.

Spend ten to fifteen minutes in this space. Then ask the space: "What percentage of light may I take back with me for my highest good?" Hear or simply know the percentage. Your percentage could be 5 percent or 20 percent. Imagine taking this increased percentage of light back to your Earth body and experiencing life from this more en-light-ened perspective.

Step 3: Returning to Your Body

When you have received all the benefit you can from this meditation, bring your spirit body back into your physical body and enjoy the feelings of a higher vibration. Do your best to remember throughout your day that you are operating with more light inside of you. Notice whether you act differently or whether the day's events bring you interesting surprises.

When you awaken the following day, say to yourself "Today I am going to live with ten percent more light!" Will your body feel differently? How do you think this increased light will translate into your everyday world? How does this light affect your relationships with your family, animal companions, and co-workers?

Go back to this meditation as often as you like for the enjoyable feelings you experience in the light and to bring back more light into your life.

Chapter 5

The Role of Beliefs in Creating Your Experience

We now begin a new chapter to further examine your beliefs. Because beliefs influence the creation of your experience, you want tools to examine and transform negative belief patterns. Therefore, included are exercises to identify your personal beliefs, how they influence your life, and how you can substitute more desirable beliefs. Prior to this, we explore how beliefs help create your life experience and how certain dominant societal beliefs are the result of the ego-mind and underlie this world of duality. Identifying and changing beliefs is one of the more challenging steps in personal transformation. Yet transforming your beliefs pays major dividends in creating a more enjoyable life.

Defining Beliefs

Beliefs are more than opinions and preferences. Unlike an opinion, such as "people who are very rich should pay a higher percentage of taxes than people who are not," or a preference, such as "I would rather have a cat as a pet than a dog," a belief is an acceptance of something as true. A belief is strongly held and rarely changes.

Often a belief is so ingrained in a person's psyche that the belief is viewed as a "fact of life." At one time, for example, people believed the sun revolved around the Earth. There are many who still believe that animals have no "soul" or do not experience pain, sorrow, or have intelligence as does man. A belief may also be so hidden in the subconscious it is not even recognized as a belief by the individual. A common example of a hidden belief is "I am not worthy." An individual may not admit or recognize this as a belief, yet their demeanor and actions say otherwise. Regardless of whether you are aware of your beliefs, they direct the choices and actions in your life and are an integral part of how your life unfolds. In other words, beliefs are at the root of your creative nature.

The Process of Creation

As a part and reflection of All That Is, you are a creator. You create your life experience and contribute to the experience of your world. Your creations are based on your beliefs about life and on how strongly you hold those beliefs; they become the foundation of what you think you can or cannot achieve. Also part of the creation process are your intentions, emotions, thoughts, words and, of course, actions. Intentions are the goals or decisions you set for yourself. These are fueled by emotions. The more strongly you feel about something or visualize what you wish to create in your mind, the more likely you are to bring your goals into fruition. Your thoughts and words also have impact and are generally a reflection of your beliefs. Since you are in a physical world, the actions you take confirm or negate your intentions. These, too, are a reflection of your beliefs.

For example, two people can come from the same disadvantaged background. While one becomes a successful businessman the other barely scrapes by. The one believes he can achieve anything he sets his mind to. With strong intention, thoughts, words, and actions that reflect that belief, he achieves his dream. The other looks around his environment and believes that only the few lucky ones can succeed. His strongly held belief can even cause him to sabotage circumstances that could otherwise help him achieve the success he believes only comes to others.

This same process of creation can help you quickly sell a house in a down market, create a new invention, expand your friendships, bring more income into your life, improve your health, and help you find a new and loving relationship. Beyond these more typical achievements in daily life, mankind has the capability of achieving feats viewed as "impossible" or "miraculous." When the Christ healed the sick, multiplied the loaves and fishes, and walked on water, he was illustrating the ability that lies within all mankind. As a creator, you have this potential that is currently only limited by strongly held beliefs to the contrary.

Limiting Beliefs Created by the Ego-Mind

Many strongly held beliefs are the result of the ego-mind's immersion in fear. As noted previously, in order to have the experience of "that which you are not," the ego-mind was necessary in order to create a world of duality or contrast—a world of "good" and "bad" and a world of "love" and "fear." To do this required three basic assumptions or beliefs: "I am separate," "There is not enough," and "I do not direct my life experience." These beliefs are secured assumptions that we hold and that influence every aspect of our lives.

A Belief in Separation

In the first assumption, the ego-mind views itself as separate from All That Is. This includes a separation from all other beings (human and otherwise) and the rest of the natural world. This belief in separation has numerous dysfunctional effects. There is a loneliness and a longing for connection brought on by this assumption. This can lead to states of depression, hopelessness, and anxiety. By seeing oneself as separate, people are easily divided into good and bad. Separation provides justification for anger, hatred, bigotry, resentment, violence, and murder, and tolerates injustice, poverty, and ignorance.

Animals and the Earth's environment also suffer from those who do not see their connection. While this core belief has allowed your inner being to have creative experiences that have increased your inner being's understanding of itself, the belief in separation now stands in the way of bringing your loving inner being forth into this physical experience. Releasing this core belief, more than any other belief, brings about your peaceful and loving nature. When you believe you are connected with all, you intuitively know your actions affect all that surrounds you. You naturally become kinder—more compassionate and understanding.

Remembering you are one with all life is an essential step in your transformation—in your re-membering with your inner being.

Exercises and meditations can assist you in experiencing a oneness with other beings and with aspects of the natural world. A very simple exercise that is available on a daily basis is to do your best to understand why an individual in your life is acting in a certain manner. Perhaps you remember how you felt about life when you were a teenager. You can put yourself in the shoes of an older person who has identified closely with his or her career or children and no longer feels useful. Seeing how poverty and neglect might lead to drug addiction can give you a more understanding view of a person who "never seems to get ahead." Using your imagination to place yourself in another's shoes helps reduce feelings of separation. As this core belief slowly dissolves, your experience of judgment and negative emotions will dissipate and your energy signature will improve markedly.

A Meditation on Experiencing Oneness with the Animal World

Another means of fostering unity consciousness is to place yourself in the consciousness of another species. The following meditation allows you to merge with an animal and experience life from its perspective. You will find wisdom, compassion, and an understanding that animals are aware of their oneness with All That Is. They live in the moment and enjoy the physical nature of the world. They have much to teach and, through these teachings, enable you to better understand your connection with them and with the One.

Step 1: Setting the Stage

As you normally do, find a quiet space where you will not be disturbed for about twenty to thirty minutes. Close your eyes, and relax. Go to your special place and call in your inner being, guides, angels, and any animal companions you wish to help you in this meditation. Then ask your spirit body to move out from your physical body while still staying attached.

Step 2: Asking the Universe to Send You an Animal

Once you see your spirit body, ask the universe to bring to you the perfect animal for your highest good. State your intention to learn more about the animal's life on Earth, what they know, why they are here in this form and anything else they wish to tell you about their experiences on Earth. Make sure to suspend any idea of what animal will come forward and let the universe choose for you.

Step 3: Communing with Your Animal

When the animal comes forward, acknowledge and thank him or her for taking the time to be with you. Ask if he/she is willing for you to join with him/her for the next half hour or so. If the animal says yes, let your spirit body merge with its body and go on a journey together. Let the animal show or tell you about its life. Learn all you can about your animal from its perspective. You may be attached to the animal or merge completely with it.

Step 4: Returning to Your Body and Recording Your Experience

When you have experienced all that your animal has to show or tell you, thank your animal for its insight and guidance. Return your spirit body to your physical body and record your experience.

A Belief in "Not Enough"

The second limiting core belief of "there is not enough" assumes that the universe itself is limited: There is not enough time, money, land, jobs, resources, and so on. This belief has justified a wide range of actions from something as small as not taking the time to exercise, play with the children or call your mother, to not giving to charity or looking for the job of your dreams. This belief in "not enough" can result in petty theft, extreme disparities in employee salaries, or even grand theft, warfare, and destruction of the environment.

"Not enough" is used by the government and accepted by the governed to justify not providing for the basic needs of the population, whether these needs are housing, education, food, energy, or health care. On the other hand, "not enough" is used less often when referring to the cost of war, policing, or prisons. When you believe in your ability to create—as an individual and as a community and in your oneness with Source, who is infinite—there is always "enough." An individual who believes there is "enough" would no longer have the need to constantly accumulate and consume. A society that believes there is "enough" would see to the basic needs of its population and, as a byproduct, would reduce the need to expend its resources on oversight, policing, prisons, and war. As with the belief in the oneness of all, a belief that there is enough provides feelings of balance, security, and peace and your energy signature is once again improved.

A Belief That "I Do Not Direct My Life Experience"

The final core belief of the ego-mind is the assumption that much of a person's experience is controlled by outside circumstances. For most of you, the concept that "you create your reality" is difficult to grasp. You can easily see how your actions impact certain aspects of daily life: one goes to school, gets a degree, and finds a job in their field. If one eats well, exercises, and takes vitamins, good health results. A person who works hard and saves their money is comfortable in retirement. It is more difficult to see how your actions impact other aspects of daily life. The explanation for this is quite complex.

Each of you is a magnificent spiritual being having a physical experience. Prior to your incarnation on Earth, your inner being set up key circumstances that provide you with the opportunity to better experience and know certain aspects of itself. Your inner being may wish to learn more about receiving from another and live a lifetime as an invalid. Through such an experience, your inner being can more fully understand patience and acceptance or how to achieve dignity and humor under trying circumstances. Your caretaker will also have the opportunity to experience patience, compassion, and understanding. There will be an exquisite dance between the two to see if they can see themselves in the other and experience the deep closeness that exists between them.

A soul may agree to live a very short life in order to provide an impetus for his or her parents to question organized religion. In so doing, the parents have the opportunity to look inside for answers as to the nature of reality, the eternal nature of the soul, and the beauty and wonder of all aspects of Life or God, even in that which appears tragic. Another soul could agree to depart this world as part of a larger tragedy and with many other souls, such as in an earthquake, flood, or holocaust. This provides humanity with the opportunity to express its compassion and kindness and recognize their bond with others. In the case of war or genocide, humanity can decide where it stands relative to that. Will each individual and society choose peace and tolerance, or will they continue to see war and violence as viable solutions?

You are a part of All That Is. As such, you draw people and circumstances to you in order to better know yourself. There are circumstances or people that are drawn to you to mirror your current vibration. This can include the angry clerk, the critical teacher, the encouraging words of the coach, and the unexpected check in the mail. Other people and circumstances are drawn to you as a reflection of your beliefs about yourself and life. If, for example, you believe that "nothing ever goes right" then you find your computer is always breaking down, the check gets lost in the mail, or the repairman does a poor job and charges too much. On the other hand, something completely unexpected happens, providing you with an opportunity to experience spontaneity or patience or even laughter and joy. All of these examples are given to illustrate that you are never a victim of circumstances. *At some level, the spiritual part of your being has reached out to another aspect of itself in order to be part of an experience that increases the understanding of the One and of Inner Being as part of the One.*

When you fully accept that you are the creator of your life, you stop resisting the circumstances of your life. In addition, you more consciously engage in creating your life experience. Those who master this easily fall into the space of the Silent Observer. The world is viewed without judgment, in wonder, with gentle humor, and with joy in the part you are playing in this grand game of Life. Knowing you are an eternal being who is capable of choosing to create a new experience draws you to your peaceful center and, again, brings your energy signature to a higher level.

Taking Stock of Life

So, how is this accomplished? What if you have lost your job? What if a divorce has left you with a much smaller income, a large stack of bills, and children who are depending upon you? What if you are disabled and have difficulty working steadily? What if you have aging parents who are relying on you or an alcoholic spouse or a special needs child? Do you view these difficulties as insurmountable, as something to be endured . . . as fate? Are you hoping that someone else will rescue you or that you will win the lottery and all will be well?

All of these circumstances can be frightening and overwhelming. However, when you believe you are the creator of your experience, that you are literally one with the Creator and all of Life, and when you understand that within the infinite universe there is always enough, you align yourself with the creative abilities of your inner being. Through an examination of your beliefs, you can achieve insight into the limiting beliefs that are keeping you from creating life circumstances that are more pleasing to you. Regardless of the situation you find yourself in, you can make your life better. The ability to create your tomorrow lies in the beliefs, thoughts, and vibration you hold today.

The Hazards of Affirmations

You can successfully achieve your desires even in dire circumstances when you evaluate what brought you to this place—those beliefs that have led to this situation. Since your beliefs are the conditional cause of your experience, take time to examine your root beliefs. Often, people are told to "think positively." They are given affirmations to say over and over that promise to lead them to a new and better life. Unfortunately, their ego-mind is filled with doubt, fear, guilt, or feelings of unworthiness even while the affirmations are dutifully repeated. These feelings echo beliefs the individual has about himself and life that are so strong that positive thinking and affirmations cannot overcome them. After a short period of being "positive" with little or no results, the individual gives up saying, "I knew this wouldn't work. Nothing good ever happens to me. I don't know why I even try." Instead, work with your inner being to explore your beliefs and expectations in greater depth.

Examining and Changing Limiting Beliefs: Three Journal Exercises

An examination of your beliefs and assumptions can occur in a number of ways. What we suggest is that you use the wisdom of your inner being to search out beliefs that are false and not in keeping with your loving, spiritual nature. Since issues pertaining to your feelings of security can cause you great dis-ease, we focus on exercises that examine beliefs relative to security, money, or your vocation. You can also use these exercises to examine limiting beliefs pertaining to health, relationships, or even your view of the world.

A Journal Exercise to Examine Beliefs Related to Security or Money

Step 1: Setting the Stage

Set aside thirty to sixty minutes of time and go to a comfortable place where you will not be disturbed. Bring your journal to record your session.

Step 2: Stating Your Intention

Make yourself comfortable. Take deep breaths and focus on relaxing and clearing your mind. State your intention—"I intend to understand my beliefs pertaining to money and my security."

Step 3: Going to Your Special Place

Close your eyes and picture yourself going to your "special place." Ask your inner being to come sit with you and help you understand your underlying beliefs as they pertain to money and security.

Step 4: Writing Down
Your List of Beliefs

When you feel completely relaxed and peaceful, open your eyes and use your journal to write a list of beliefs related to security or money. Write down whatever comes to mind as quickly as possible. Don't stop to think. Instead, listen and write. If you get a belief or comment you do not understand, ask for further clarification. Societal views such as "money is the root of all evil" or something your parents said like "Whenever I get ahead, something always happens to take it away" are common examples.

Step 5: Picking One Belief
for Further Exploration

Once you have your list, pick one of the beliefs or comments to explore further. On a separate page in your journal, write this belief at the top. Below that, begin writing what comes to mind in terms of where this belief originated for you and how strongly you have held on to it. Then write your impressions as to the effects this belief has had in your life. How has this belief colored your views of yourself, your spouse, parents, or friends? What evidence exists in your life that shows how this belief resulted in your current situation? Do you hold other beliefs that serve to counter this belief somewhat? What are they?

Step 6: Examining the Belief

After you have written all that comes to you on this subject, examine how this belief may be false. For example, if the belief is that "money is the root of all evil," begin writing all the ways in which this belief is not *true. What kinds of things would you do if you had a large amount of money? Would it be evil to have a nice home, plenty of food, pretty clothes? What would be the beneficial uses of money for you, your family, and your community? You might respond with "money would provide me with freedom to pursue the type of work that would bring me joy." "Money would allow me to hire many workers who could fix my house, thus providing jobs in the community." "Money would allow me to be more generous to the community charities I support or help me retrofit my home or buy a more fuel efficient vehicle to help the environment"—and so on.*

Step 7: Preparing a New Belief

When you have completed this list, prepare a new belief that would substitute for the old belief, such as "Money is a neutral form of exchange that, when used in a loving manner, can be very beneficial." Then go back to your inner being and ask his or her help in substituting this belief in your life.

Changing Beliefs is Hard Work

Give yourself time to tackle each of your other beliefs in the same way until you have fully examined all of your beliefs. Although this may seem time-consuming, its impact can be profound and long-lasting. It took decades to build the false self or that part of you that does not reflect your inner being. A committed effort, therefore, is required on your part to dismantle the false self. Yet the time will be well spent!

You are not conscious of many of these beliefs much of the time, yet they affect your life and your creations. If you attempt to focus positively on finding work that you enjoy and, at the same time, believe that such work will not allow you sufficient income to support you and your family, you block a change in career that is both creatively and financially supportive. You may be clear in affirming what you want and still find that the universe cannot deliver because your strongly held beliefs are blocking that which you desire. By exploring these beliefs, where they come from and how they play out in your life, and by substituting new beliefs and fully imagining how they would improve your life, you will be ready to work with your inner being to create what you truly want. As you do your journal work on a number of the limiting beliefs that turned up, you will also find underlying beliefs such as "I am not worthy" cropping up throughout as well. These underlying beliefs are the most difficult to change. Nevertheless, as you change the initial beliefs and see this impact on your life, your belief in your self-worth and ability to create your experience will slowly shift also.

Using the Journal Belief Exercise with Others

Another way to examine your beliefs is to do this exercise with your spouse or friends in a workshop setting. After completing each step, you can take time to share your insights with the other person or the group. Many of you have similar beliefs among you, and bringing them out in the open for discussion helps everyone. You find you are not alone in this experience, especially since many people have similar cultural, geographic, and religious backgrounds. Furthermore, as one individual reports his or her beliefs, this recitation may trigger in you a recognition of similar beliefs you did not previously remember or acknowledge.

You could even practice together by taking one of the group beliefs, modifying it, and then making the new belief part of your morning exercise to set the tone of your day.

Use the new belief about money or a perfect job to imagine how good your life would be if this belief were an integral part of your day. After a couple of weeks of this, come back together and report to each other how this exercise has affected your lives or outlook. If you follow this process each day, you will be pleasantly surprised by the results.

Using the Journal Belief Exercise to Monitor Your Words and Thoughts

A third means of exploring your beliefs is to monitor what you say or even what goes on in your mind as you go about each day. This provides insight into your beliefs and helps you understand what you focus on each day and how these beliefs affect your vibration. If you say things like "I can't afford that" or "I hate paying bills" or "I hate my job" or "Nothing ever works out for me" or "I can never get ahead" or any number of similar statements, know they reflect your beliefs and are setting the stage for your life experience.

Keep a small notebook with you for two or three weeks. When you make or think a negative statement that pertains to your basic needs, write that statement down. At the end of this period, notice the statements that you say or think most often. To explore these statements more thoroughly and release them from your mind, conduct a similar process as that explained in our first belief journal exercise.

Step 1: Recording Statements Pertaining to Security

For two or three weeks, write down in a small notebook those thoughts and words that pertain to issues of security. At the end of that time, summarize them so that you have a listing of your most often expressed statements.

Step 2: Setting the Stage

Set aside thirty to sixty minutes of time and go to a comfortable place where you will not be disturbed. Bring your journal to record your session.

Step 3: Stating Your Intention

Make yourself comfortable. Take deep breaths and focus on relaxing and clearing your mind. State your intention: "I intend to understand how my words and thoughts are influencing my life experience. I wish to clearly understand the beliefs behind these words relating to money and my security and how they are affecting my life."

Step 4: Going to Your Special Place

Close your eyes and picture yourself going to your "special place." Ask your inner being to come sit with you and help you understand your underlying beliefs as they pertain to money and security.

Step 5: Focusing on One of the Statements on Your List

After you have enjoyed sufficient time with your inner being, open your eyes. Take one of the statements on your list and ask your inner being to help you understand the underlying beliefs behind that statement.

Step 6: Listing the Underlying Beliefs of Your Chosen Statement

Underneath the first statement on your list, write down the belief or beliefs that pertain to the statement you have chosen to address.

Step 7: Examining Each Belief

For each belief, write down the origin of this belief. Answer the following questions about this belief: How has this belief affected your life (i.e., Your views of yourself and others, what you have observed as the effect of this belief on your security or financial situation, or your willingness to be generous or to take risks, etc.)? What about this belief is false? What would your life be like if this belief were not true?

Step 8: Creating a New Belief

Create a new positive belief to substitute for the old belief and write the new belief down. Imagine if this new belief were now true for you and how your life would change. When you imagine this new life, explore the experience thoroughly through joyful emotions and vivid visualizations. This will help anchor the new belief within your being.

Step 9: Asking for Help

Ask your inner being for help in incorporating this new belief into your life.

Determining the Validity and Usefulness of a Belief

Examining your beliefs and changing them is hard work, for many of the beliefs or underlying assumptions of your life are not readily apparent. In fact, certain beliefs you do not see as beliefs. Rather, these beliefs are viewed as truisms of life. You have held them so long, you no longer notice them and your experience bears them out. What you will notice is when you are thinking or talking about them, you feel bad. Think of this feeling as an indicator of vibration, which it is.

When you are uncomfortable, uneasy, discouraged, scared, hopeless, powerless, or angry, this indicates you are vibrating at a lower frequency and are out of sync with your inner being. However, these more negative feelings have a positive aspect in that they encourage you to *question and evaluate the beliefs behind the feeling.* As you become more aware of your beliefs and use your emotions as your guide, you more easily release them and bring your inner being forward so that your predominant feelings are ones of peace, appreciation, and joy. The more you reside in this higher vibrational state, substituting more positive beliefs becomes easier and you create the life of abundance and creativity that you seek.

Chapter 6

Love: The Signature of Source

Thus far, we have discussed the nature of your true self and why your inner being chose this challenging Earth experience. You can now contact the wisdom of your inner being and the creative ability that lies within you. You also know that you use the creative process every day whether you are aware of how you create your experience or not. We have reviewed a variety of methods to raise your vibration or energy signature, and exercises have been provided to address daily difficulties, improve relationships, and prepare for and review each day. You now better understand the role of beliefs as they affect your energy signature and life experience, and how to change these beliefs. All of these exercises help increase your vibration and feelings of well-being and assist you to more often reside in the love of your inner being.

Before you can fully express your inner being through your love for others, however, an appreciation and love of self is needed. Although not an easy task, once achieved, you will have accomplished your goal of bringing your inner being into your daily experience. With a complete love of self comes a love of all beings and all of life.

In this chapter, you will closely examine the events and people in your life that had a significant impact on how you view yourself. Through a process designed to release the traumas and hurts you carry forward, you pave the way toward unconditional love of your precious self. New memories can be established, along with a final release and forgiveness of self and others. By working with your inner being you will understand the many benefits that accrued from the experiences that have contributed to who you are today. This is important work that will bring out your peaceful and loving nature.

Observing and Learning from Life

Loving yourself is the most natural state of your being. Although this state of being is relatively rare in the world today, to be in this state of self-love is to be "enlightened" or freed from the fear-based ego-mind. This is what you came into this time and place to do and what many of you have been working hard to achieve much of your lives. This path has not been easy. Fortunately, as you raise your energy signature along with that of the world, your efforts to express that higher part of you will become easier and more joyful and you will fall in love with your precious self.

In this time of rapid change, you and your inner being are more often bringing people and events into your experience that provide the opportunity to understand and release that which stands in the way of loving yourself. These situations can range from a serious argument with a friend or the loss of a job, home, or spouse, to the stubbing of a toe, worry about what others think of you, or how you react when you drop and break a dish.

Any of these circumstances can challenge you to examine that which keeps you from your peaceful center . . . that part of you that is affected by that which is not love and that reveals itself as anger, fear, impatience, judgment, resentment, and so on. As you take the time to examine what is behind your reaction to any of these circumstances, your new understanding can help you break the habitual ego reaction and you begin to see life through the lens of love, acceptance, and understanding. So do not be discouraged if life seems to be a bit more uncomfortable or hectic. Life's chaos is simply your inner being urging you to address any remaining barriers to loving yourself and all of life. You are on the right path and all is well.

Uncovering the Barriers to Self-Love

Using the journal exercises in the last chapter on beliefs is an excellent first step in exploring the fear-based roots of your reactions to life's challenges and is not unlike the peeling of an onion. First a belief or set of beliefs is evaluated and eventually understood to be false. You see more clearly that these beliefs act as barriers to a more peaceful and pleasing life.

As the process of evaluation continues, the core beliefs of the fear-based ego-mind are revealed: "I am separate," "There is not enough" and "I do not direct my life experience." Such beliefs, as we have seen, engender feelings of isolation and powerlessness. As we continue to peel the onion of beliefs, we get to those that most directly relate to the love of self. These beliefs include: "I am not worthy of love (whether this be from others or from God)" and, ultimately, "I am not an eternal being connected to a benevolent and loving universe."

These underlying beliefs, of course, came from the decision of mankind to play in a world of duality by forgetting the magnificence of their being. Without this memory, a new soul entering this world easily falls into fear. This is particularly true when those around the newly born act in ways not consistent with their loving inner being.

Many people have had experiences as a young child that resulted in feelings of helplessness, questions of self-worth, or even victimhood. Unfortunately, many have difficulty in releasing these memories and emotions, and they become a lens through which life is viewed. As a means of protection, the individual separates himself from those involved in these unpleasant experiences, identifying people as good or bad. The individual can also experience personal guilt or unworthiness for the part he or she played in the traumatic event. To make this more complicated, as a multi-dimensional being, significant traumas in other lifetimes can bleed through and trigger prejudices against certain people or classes of people or result in fears that have no identifiable origin in this lifetime.

Regardless of the origin of these beliefs, you can tap into your wise inner being and dig into the uncomfortable feeling or belief and re-visit the trauma that is causing the pain and distortion of experience. Releasing the pain associated with the traumatic event then becomes possible. New experiences or memories can be created and put in the place of the painful memory. Identifying the higher purpose of the event from the perspective of your inner being adds to the healing process, as does a broader perspective on the part others played in the event. With this new way of viewing the event and the creation of a better memory, you will release and forgive those involved. Through addressing and releasing the core beliefs that have been used by your inner being to experience this fascinating world of duality, you find it easier to see or know your inner being and that of others. Although these traumatic events may have been very difficult and painful, all experience is used by each person's inner being to better know itself. When a person integrates this wisdom, his life is viewed with benevolence, love, and gentle humor. When you free yourself from the weight of a painful past, en-*light*-enment will be the happy result.

A Journaling Exercise to Release Past Trauma

To assist you in releasing a traumatic childhood or specific event, here is a simple journaling process to access the wisdom of your inner being. Take as much time as you need and use the exercise for any number of memories that cause you pain, embarrassment, or vague discomfort. Each release brings you closer to your goal of self-love.

Step 1: Setting the Stage and Grounding

As always, seek a quiet and peaceful spot where you can be undisturbed for forty-five to sixty minutes. Bring your journal. Once you are relaxed and comfortable, ground yourself by extending the core of your being deep into the Earth below you. This gives you a sense of comfort and being in the present moment. If you wish, picture yourself sitting next to a large rock wall or see your legs surrounded and grounded by tree roots that go far into the Earth. Breathe with the tree and relax even further.

Step 2: Going to Your Special Place

Go to your special place and meet your inner being. State your intention to release the past issues that are keeping you from joyfully and fully living in the present. Ask for the assistance of your guides, angels, and any other archangels or ascended beings with whom you have great admiration.

Step 3: Writing a Letter to Your Inner Being

When you have completed this phase and are feeling comfort from all these beautiful beings, open your eyes and take out your journal. Begin writing a letter to your inner being ("Dear Inner Being . . ."). Start at the beginning, telling him or her what you believe happened in your life that has contributed toward your unhappiness, feelings of unworthiness, or doubt that you are lovable. Take as long as you need. Write down any questions that come to mind.

Step 4: Asking Your Inner Being for Its Wisdom

After you have expressed what you perceived to have happened, any emotions you felt at the time, as well as those feelings you still hold, ask your inner being and spiritual helpers to give you the highest perspective of your experience, keeping in mind these questions as you do so:

- *Why did I choose to create this experience? (Remember, you are the creator of your experience.)*

- *What role did others play in this event to assist me in my personal growth?*

- *How did this experience lead to my personal growth and the raising of my vibration?*

Before you undertake this process do your best to release all expectations. Go even deeper into a relaxed state. Start your letter from your inner being ("Dearest Beloved . . .") and write whatever comes to you in answer to your questions. Answers that are loving, insightful, and leave you feeling uplifted are from your inner being. Critical, negative, unforgiving, or fear-based answers come from the ego-mind. If that should occur, put your journal aside for another time. Return to the process when you are ready.

Step 5: Creating a New Memory

If you are dealing with a traumatic memory, ask your inner being to assist you in creating, through your imagination, a more pleasant and preferred memory to take the place of the actual memory.

Once again, place yourself in a relaxed state and close your eyes. Create a detailed picture of a new, preferred memory. Breathe and take your time. Place yourself in this new memory by using your feelings—see yourself smiling, experience a sense of safety and security, happiness, and satisfaction. Keep breathing and allow this preferred memory to permeate your being until this new memory overwrites the old. Bring this new memory up in your meditations as often as you like in order to fully anchor this memory into your being.

Step 6: Releasing and Forgiving

The final step in this process involves release and forgiveness. Ask your inner being to show you the inner beings or higher selves of those who may have hurt you. See their bright light and oneness with Source. Imagine them surrounded, as are you, by their guides and guardian angels. See how the light of their inner being connects and merges with the light of their guides, angels, and your inner being. Ask to deeply understand the truism that all are connected to and a part of God.

Stay in this space of oneness.

Allow for your compassion and understanding to result in a state of forgiveness. Forgive others for their misdeeds. Forgive yourself for any misperceptions you may have had, while experiencing gratitude for what you learned. Gently remind yourself that you have created your experiences for reasons of personal growth, the highest of which is to extend your love to all beings and to recognize that all experiences are part of Source experiencing Source. Know that when you forgive the "unforgiveable," you are expressing unconditional love and that unconditional love is the truest definition of love.

Step 7: Returning from the Meditative State

When you are done with this last portion of releasing and forgiving, slowly bring yourself out of your meditative state. Thank your inner being and other spiritual helpers. Later, as you touch base through a review of your writings, further release will occur until you no longer identify yourself as a victim of your past and, instead, have a greater sense of peace and well-being.

Accessing Past Lives for Release

Since you are multi-dimensional beings who have spent many and various lives on Earth throughout time, your present life is sometimes affected by a difficult past life. A traumatic injury or death in a life as a soldier could cause an otherwise inexplicable back or neck pain. If you have a reaction with an individual you just met that is either immediately satisfying or very uncomfortable, this reaction of yours may have its origin in another lifetime. An association with animals or children may bring up a deep but unexplained sorrow.

The following simple meditation can help you revisit a scene from a past or even a future life, which will provide you with insight and release in this life. You may believe you are just "imagining" a past life. Yet we assure you that your inner being talks with you most effectively through your imagination. Think! If there is something troubling you and the reason is not readily apparent, then use this meditation and see what the "gazing glass" has to show you.

Meditation to See the Influence of Past Lives on the Present Life

Step 1: Setting the Stage

Take fifteen to thirty minutes and go to a place where you will not be disturbed. Breathe deeply and enter into a relaxed state. Have an issue in mind for which you would like greater clarity.

Step 2: Looking into the Gazing Glass

See yourself going into a large and deep cave. After walking for a bit, you come to a large lake. There is a soft light that allows you to see. Along the lake, you find a comfortable spot where you can sit at the edge of the lake. As you sit watching the lake, notice that the top of the lake resembles a gazing glass. In the glass-like mirror of the lake, you now see images of your life. It can be past or future images of your current life, images of past lives, or images of your future lives. If you are puzzled as to why this particular past life has arisen relative to your concern, ask your inner being for clarification. This clarification may happen right away or much later when your mind is at rest.

Step 3: Relaxing in the Water

After your experience with the gazing glass, you may decide to go into the water. The water is warm and clear. Become like a dolphin or turtle or any aquatic fish or mammal that assists you in breathing underwater or simply know that you can breathe underwater. Enjoy your warm swim and the quiet beauty of the underwater world. Create any light that may assist you. Stay in this relaxing, womb-like water until you are ready to leave.

Step 4: Returning to Your Room and Recording Your Experience

When you have finished with the gazing glass and the beauty of the underwater world, slowly return to your room and enjoy your relaxed state. Record your experience. Notice over time whether this meditation has provided a release or a better understanding of whatever issue was of concern.

Imprinting Authentic Love into Your Energy Signature

Time and effort are necessary to elevate your energy signature to that of your inner being. Fortunately, you discover that each step taken makes the next step easier. As you peel away the armor of your ego-mind, which has done its best to protect you from its perception of a fear-based world, you see the world through new eyes, easily accepting others *as they are.* You recognize that the divine aspect of the other is connected to Source and to you.

With this energy signature of authentic love you view others with kindness. When you approach them by seeing the highest part of who they are and by accepting their humanity (their strengths and weaknesses), you love them unconditionally. This does not mean you must approve of all their actions or not take steps when they seek to harm others or themselves. It means you neither judge nor condemn them but, rather, view their actions with understanding and compassion.

There but by the Grace of God

Throughout time, each of you has been both the villain and heroine, killer and victim, abuser and the abused, rich and poor, male and female, compassionate and one without compassion, judge and the judged, famous and obscure, and everything in between. Your personal struggles become the basis of your understanding and compassion. As you look closely at your own life, you know there have been times when you have struck out in anger, said things you regretted, caused harm to an animal, or damaged Mother

Earth. Taking a broader perspective, recognize that as an eternal being you have experienced numerous lives on this beloved planet of contrasts in which you have played many parts. Beyond all that is the profound understanding that nothing is separate from the One and all that you experience is experienced by the One. So, too, the experience of the All is *your* experience. When you condemn another, you condemn yourself. By condemning another, you condemn God or that which is Life. When you deeply love your own being you will express the same love for all beings.

Making Change Easy

If all of this sounds too overwhelming or the path of "saints" and not that of ordinary people, we say to each of you that the largest part of you is already at this loving place. Like a very wet dog, you are in the process of shaking off all that is not love. You are engaged in this process of personal growth and transformation right now and many others are engaged with you. The process itself is simple. What is your energy signature at this moment? If what you are saying and doing gives you satisfaction, if you are laughing, playing, or dancing with joy, if you are peaceful and content, if you are grateful for what is before you, then you have a raised energy signature and you are resonating with your inner being. If you are uncomfortable with what you are saying and doing, if you are angry, resentful, jealous, or depressed, if you are dissatisfied and not happy with what you have, then your energy signature is low and is resonating with the ego-mind.

Your guidance system is unerring, so take the time to notice this guidance system and use the various techniques we provide to bring yourself back to your peaceful center.

Above all, remember that life on Earth is not primarily a grueling learning experience. Life is a means for you to play, to en-*joy*, to experience beauty and wonder in the smallest of things. You may try a technique that others have used to remind themselves to alter their attitude. Put a rubber band on your wrist and when your perspective of life has taken a downward dive, snap the rubber band as a reminder to see life through the lens of love. There is always something wondrous surrounding you, even if it is only the realization that you are a being with thoughts, senses, and movement.

Is that not amazing? Take that moment to become acutely aware of your surroundings and look around you as if for the first time. Snap that rubber band as many times as needed until you no longer require a reminder. This path will lead you back to the playground of life that many of you experienced as children. When you find yourself smiling and laughing more often, that will be your inner being saying . . . ."This is what your life was meant to be. Good job!"

Chapter 7

The World as Your Playground

Much of the material provided thus far has addressed how to use the mind and the imagination to release past trauma, limiting beliefs, and worrisome projections into the future. All of these are aspects of the ego-mind that color your perception and keep you from being completely engaged in life. In this chapter we help you observe and deactivate the overactive mind and use your marvelous physical senses to interact with your world as a playground rather than a battlefield. Many master teachers, including Eckhart Tolle, would say this is about "being in the moment," which is also about being "out of the mind."

The Mind In Its Natural State

The human form is a marvelous vehicle with which to experience this physical world. The physical body enjoys the senses of sight, touch, taste, smell, and hearing. The mind, in its natural state, observes and takes pleasure in the solving of puzzles and the inventing of new ways of doing things as part of its creative nature. The emotions arising out of this state of natural being are joy, peace, and deep satisfaction. When you are in this natural state of being, you are in a state of timelessness . . . you are a human *being*.

The Development of the Ego-Mind

In society today this state of "being" is most often present in very young children who have not yet absorbed the cultural and familial fears of the ego-mind. If you watch how these children interact with life, you notice they reside in the moment and are keenly aware of their surroundings.

As they age, you begin to see the workings of the ego-mind. A harsh word is remembered and action is taken to avoid such a painful interaction again. Promises of a field trip, birthday party, or other celebration may cause the young child to develop yearnings or a sense of anticipation that keeps them from enjoying what they are doing in the present moment. As they grow into adults, they become more acutely aware of "time," constantly referring to the clock as they go about their day. While the occasional reference to the clock is a necessary part of modern culture, dwelling on the loss of time or feeling hurried and constantly watching the clock is one way the ego-mind keeps from being in the now.

Another aspect of the ego-mind is its ongoing stream of conversation—evaluating what is currently happening against a painful past event, judging the actions of others as a means of being "better than" (or separate from), and anticipating a future event with either dread or pleasure. The experience of the "now" or of the life that is currently unfolding is consequently obscured.

The constant chattering of the mind is not the mind's natural state. This chatter, however, is the norm for most people today. The chattering mind varies only in degree from person to person. In previous chapters we have shown how you can observe this chatter and gain an understanding of the underlying beliefs that direct your experience. Such observation also helps you understand how your current life is affected by painful past events. By bringing these beliefs and past events into your conscious knowing, you can release the unconscious hold they have on you.

Finding Release from the Ego-Mind

As you gain release from past traumas and dysfunctional beliefs, you begin to have moments when the mind is silent. Many will naturally experience this when they are engaged in a creative endeavor, such as art, music, or dance. In these cases, the mind is involved in the creative aspects of the activity and the chatter is silenced. This does not mean the ego-mind cannot be present, for the opportunity always exists for fear and judgment to enter into the creative process. Still, when a person is fully engaged in their activity or in the "zone" that athletes speak of, the ego-mind is absent. You may find relief from the chattering mind by petting your cat, being struck by the beauty of a rainbow, or actively tasting and enjoying the first ice-cream cone of the summer. What all of these examples have in common are the use and awareness of your physical senses without the running commentary of the chattering mind.

For most, these instances of the silent mind are fleeting moments that go unnoticed. Also not noticed is the ongoing commentary that is the more normal state of mind. Therefore, your first and most basic step toward quieting the mind is to observe your thoughts as an outside observer would. *Listen to your mind.* The commentary could be about something your spouse said or about counting the number of items in a person's grocery cart who is in front of you in the speed lane. Your mind could be fuming over someone going slow in the passing lane or judging the size of the cake being eaten by a person who is overweight. Perhaps the chattering mind will contemplate what you will be doing over the weekend or how nice things will be when you go on vacation. A news article on the falling prices in the housing market could set your mind on bleak scenarios relative to your retirement.

All of you recognize many of these thoughts, yet you do not experience them as unusual or dysfunctional. Mostly, you do not notice them at all. Once you do begin to observe your thoughts, you can evaluate and place their origin (i.e., "I am separate," or "I am afraid I will be hurt again") and recognize that your ego-mind is keeping you from being in and surrendering to that which is occurring in the now moment.

The chattering mind is a long-standing habit that has been largely unconscious. Therefore, effort and time are required to quiet the mind. Use the tool of intention to assist you—"*Today I will notice what my mind is saying and determine what lies behind the commentary. I will then turn my attention to what is occurring in the present moment without judgment. I will observe my mind at rest.*" This may be difficult at first, but as you bring these thoughts to the light of conscious realization, they occur less often. Then the resting mind can become your natural and "normal" state of being.

Resisting Life

The concept of surrender is one that is viewed negatively in society. Yet if you surrender to that which appears before you in life, you are simply accepting what is happening and living that experience until you choose a different experience. Instead, most individuals are often in a state of resistance.

Consider how you typically go about your day. Are you happy to arise in the morning or do you resist getting out of bed? Do you go to work with great anticipation and joy or would you rather be somewhere else? When you sit down to eat, are you happy and grateful for your food or would you rather be eating something else? If your child wants attention or would like you to play with her, do you relish the opportunity or do you feel annoyed because of all the other things you are pressured to address? Do you do your tasks, such as cooking or cleaning, with joy or with resistance or resentment? Even events you might look forward to can be tainted by the resistance caused by judgment or worry. For example, you may view a long-anticipated vacation as less than satisfactory because all was not as expected or because much of the time is spent worrying about what is happening at home.

All of these instances are judgments of the ego-mind. The now moment is unsatisfactory and the mind is attached to something the mind would rather be doing. Surrendering to or acceptance of the moment quiets the ego-mind and helps you to peacefully and actively participate in your life.

By its nature, resistance takes effort and drains your energy signature. The cumulative effects of resistance are fatigue and stress, which often lead to feelings of being hurried and dissatisfied. In a nutshell, when a person resists life, he or she is out of the flow of life. To flow with life, replace the ego-mind's resistance with acceptance, satisfaction, wonder, and even curiosity. These are all states of "being." Be accepting, be satisfied, be curious, or be in wonder of your world.

If there is an activity you have committed to do, whether the activity is simple or complex, consider all its desirable aspects (be satisfied). Appreciate the sunrise in the morning and greet the new day with positive anticipation (be in wonder). At work you can do your best to enjoy the challenge of your work assignments and look for different ways of approaching the project (be curious). If your car has a flat tire, the cat has barfed up a fur ball, or the new recipe didn't quite turn out as expected, smile and simply do what you need to do (be accepting). There is no reward in resisting the activity; resistance only moves you from your peaceful center.

In each of these activities, there is a state of acceptance or surrender. With this acceptance, you can use your senses to enhance the experience, perhaps exploring aspects you never have before. When you are without judgment, you are not resisting life and, consequently, you are able to peacefully flow with life. You are focused in the moment and on the activity at hand. You are a human who is *being*.

Life is a Game—Go Play!

The ego-mind immersed in fear acts as a damper or significant governor on your life (i.e., allowing your "car" to go only so fast). En*light*enment is the casting off of this governor, freeing you to fully participate in every moment in this beautiful world you have chosen to experience. Once you have taken the important step of noticing the dialogue in your mind, you will be living life in the present moment. The next step is to immerse yourself in the juiciness of that which is life.

You are here as a physical being in order to experience and play with the physical world. So *begin with the satisfying aspects of what you are doing.* Look at what you are doing as if for the first time or last time. Involve all of your wonderful physical senses. What do you hear? Are you listening to the music in which all of the instruments blend seamlessly together? What about the laughter of your young child or the ticking of a clock? Can you feel the energy behind the howl of a powerful wind; the joy behind the lyrical song of the bird; or the strength and purity that is in the music of a refreshing stream? Can you smell the wet earth; the cooking of an aromatic soup or pie; the coat of a wet but beloved dog? When was the last time you "stopped to smell the roses?" What about the scent of your shampoo or the fragrant smell of your freshly bathed baby? What about the sensitivity of your skin—do you experience warmth from the dishwater; the soft blowing of the wind in your hair; your body against the newly washed sheets on your bed?

Can you identify with the muscles in your body? Are you enjoying a brisk walk and how your body responds to your unconscious commands? When was the last time you actually walked through the rain or let the snowflakes fall on your tongue? What do you see before you? What color is the water today? Is the ocean a deep gray, reflecting an angry sky? Is it multi-colored as the sun sets? Or is the sea bright blue, alive with sparkling lights reflecting a clear and glorious day? What about that tiny bird at your feeder—the one you hardly ever notice? Even the most common of birds is exquisite in its design, coloring, and movement.

When you place yourself on this path of using all your physical senses, you open yourself up to the broader senses of your inner being. As you experience the deer, the flower, the bird, or the tree, you become acutely aware of their life force. Their love, life force, and beauty will bowl you over!

A Walking Meditation

To gain experience with engaging all of your senses, take a "walking meditation," allowing your inner being to peek out and enjoy the physical world.

Step 1: Going to a Place in Nature

Find a favorite park, field, woods, beach, stream, or lake and walk for about thirty minutes to an hour. If you walk with another, agree together that the walk will be in silence.

Step 2: Being Aware

- *Be aware of each footfall on the ground—the lifting and raising of the foot and the landing of the foot on the ground. This will cause your steps to be slower. Notice the texture of the ground. Experience the particles under your feet being compressed with each step and then open and release as you leave each spot.*

- *Be aware of each breath as you breathe in and out naturally.*

- *As you walk, turn your attention to the life around you, engaging all your senses. Smell the air, notice the direction of the wind and identify the texture of the air (is the air humid or dry?). With each step, notice the sounds around you—the songs of birds, neighbors, dogs barking, or the sounds of the water or cars driving by. When judgment arises, release it on the out breath and practice an acceptance for all sounds and sights.*

- *If you want to rest, sit down and rest.*

Step 3: Having a Picnic

If you like, prepare food to take on your walk. Long ago, people would prepare and eat their food outdoors. Eating outdoors will bring up past memories and create new ones. Notice how eating outdoors affects your experiences of hunger and taste. You may find your enjoyment of the food greatly enhanced when eating outdoors.

Living Your Life

Life is good, for life is All That Is! This is your *game*—your *creation!* Only you can make life enjoyable. All this occurs with a gentle shift in perspective. And, when you get temporarily lost again in the mind, simply notice that and then turn your attention to that which you are doing, using all your senses to bring your experiences into greater clarity and joy. If you approach this change of habit as an interesting and challenging game, the world will soon be your playground. You will be a *conscious* creator, creating your life from a high vibration. You will be as you were meant to be—a human *being*.

Chapter 8

Healing the Body

For many individuals, little thought is given to their body unless something goes seriously wrong with it. When sickness occurs, the individual often looks to sources outside himself or herself for the causes of illness. Whether the problem is an accident, virus, or chronic disease, the individual believes he has relatively little responsibility for the condition or outcome. From our perspective (i.e., that of the Pegasus Group) we see more clearly the ultimate *potential* of the body as directed by your inner being.

In this chapter we will help you understand the reasons your inner being might have chosen your body. Furthermore, you will gain insight as to how the body is affected by the ego-mind and how your beliefs relate to the health of the body. We discuss how the body is used by your inner being to get your attention and help you in your personal growth. Finally, we provide guidance for listening to your body and nurturing it with your love and appreciation. Although we wish to be clear that you do not consciously create the sickness and dysfunctions in your body, we would like you to understand that you have a much greater ability to affect the body than you now believe. In the future, through changing beliefs and a much higher energy signature, you will be able to avoid or overcome much of the disease that seems inevitable today. We look forward to that happier future as, we are sure, do you.

The Uses and Potential of the Human Body

The state of your physical body is dependent upon many divergent factors. First, before you came into the physical world, you chose a body with certain characteristics in order to carry out specific goals or challenges you set for yourself, and/or as a means of helping others meet their goals or challenges. For instance, a soul that wanted to view the physical world from a completely different perspective, that wanted to learn how to receive and be dependent upon others, and/or who wanted to help others learn about unconditional love, might come into this world with severe developmental or physical challenges. Another soul might have a frail physical body so it could live an intellectually dominated life. Yet another would come into a very athletic body with a high motivation to achieve in that area or come into a body and home situation where its inner being could hone its musical abilities.

Regardless, most of you come into physical bodies that work amazingly well and have high degrees of energy, acute sensory perception, and good intellectual capacity. These bodies are meant to and are capable of living long, active, and healthy lives. Your cells have wonderful powers of regeneration. Unfortunately, your personal and broader environment has had an adverse impact upon the well-being and longevity of most beings living on the planet.

While your bodies are resilient and can take a great deal of negativity over what appears to be long periods of time, the body is actually meant to live in vibrant health and well-being for significantly longer periods of time than is presently the case. As you bring your inner being more and more into your daily experience, your body will respond positively. The first thing that happens is that further deterioration of your body is lessened. You will notice greater levels of energy and find you are more refreshed after sleeping. Over time, you will be able to reflect the peace and love of your inner being for longer periods of time. By directing your thoughts while in this higher state of peace, you can reverse damage that has been inflicted on the body by past bouts of worry and stress. Should you reach the point of residing in this higher state of being most of the time, significant healing is possible. Yet this significant healing can occur only if you believe this to be the case and if you can overcome the dominant thought patterns of society.

Extracting The Invisible Elephant in the World's Living Room

The dominant societal beliefs you have adopted as *truths* are what affect your physical state the most. The "elephant in the room," is the belief in the relatively rapid aging and deterioration of the body. Slowly, you see this belief being challenged. You have professional athletes who are still performing at peak performance in their forties or later. You have termed what was previously considered "old age" as the new forties or fifties for people who are much older. Still, this belief in the effects of aging is undeniable by most people today. Each decade that marks your birth affects your conscious and unconscious expectations, and your body shows its effects. Getting beyond this particular belief barrier will require a shift in the beliefs of individuals and society—beliefs that relate to the unlimited spiritual nature of humanity and how that can ultimately be expressed in this physical world.

As certain key belief structures change, they will eventually lead the way to the questioning and dismantling of other beliefs, such as this one on aging. For example, the belief that "you create your reality or experience" has been posited by masters throughout time. More recently this belief has become more broadly accepted.

As individuals continue to assimilate this belief that they create their reality, they are doing so to the extent of their comfort zone. At first they may allow themselves to manifest a convenient parking space or have an unusually light traffic day when they are late to a meeting. After a time, they might easily procure a slot in a highly desirable day care center for their child, find that perfect contractor in a competitive market, or run across the ideal outfit on sale for that wedding they plan to attend. As they gain experience and allow for the possibility of bigger results, money comes in unexpected ways, relationships are repaired, they meet an old friend who connects them to that perfect job, or their house sells for a great price in a down market. All of these situations are still within most people's comfort zone. Nevertheless, these manifestations are setting the stage for grander "miracles" that only a relatively few beings and ascended masters have achieved. These include such achievements as the walking on water, bi-location, the direct manifestation of food, *and the healing of disease.*

Our point is that societal beliefs are quite limited at this time *in light of the unlimited nature of your true being.* A shift in the beliefs of a sufficient number of people regarding their potential as creators will be necessary so that others can see and then admit such possibilities in themselves. When this societal shift in belief occurs, and as the population increases its energy signature (thus reducing the significant stress and drain on the body), mankind will live longer and more vigorous lives.

In the meantime, there are many other societal beliefs that are like "running commentary," affecting your personal belief structure as well as your expectations. For example, a diagnosis of "cancer" or "AIDS" is often viewed as a death sentence. This is especially the case when a person in authority, such as the individual's physician, gives a prognosis of certain death or predicts an inevitable recurrence of the disease after a period of treatment. The few people who overcome this prognostication are seen as anomalies and do not shake the physician's firm belief in the patient's imminent demise—a belief that is reaffirmed for the physician many times through his or her experience with other patients. From the perspective of the Pegasus Group, we see that the belief regarding the illness itself and the expectation of what the health care system can achieve have a profound effect on the outcome. And, although the individual may have a strong will to live and does his or her best to "fight the good fight," their underlying and even unconscious beliefs hinder or effectively negate their innate ability to heal themselves.

At the core of this dilemma is the identification with the disease to the detriment of the natural well-being of the body. Remember that the universal law of creation is *"upon that which you focus, you create."* This is so whether you place your attention upon that which is desired or that which is feared and unwanted. We call this a dilemma because you often walk a fine line. One person could be buoyed by a healthy lifestyle because they see themselves becoming healthier and more vital and firmly believe this to be the case. Another person could be an avid exerciser and careful with what he eats, yet be driven to do these things because of a father who died young and a fear that the same thing could happen to him.

The first person wishes to achieve optimum health and well-being. The second person wishes to avoid illness and death. Given the nature of the creative process, we suggest that when you make a lifestyle change to improve your health, you see the change as contributing to your greater well-being and not as a disagreeable means of avoiding the disease or death that you fear. The body listens to the dominant belief!

The Role of Sickness in the World

Sickness has been a creation of humanity and has served many useful purposes by allowing a wide range of emotions and experiences that have contributed to humanity's spiritual growth. The form that illness has taken throughout time has changed, as has the method of treatment. Even though the types of diseases have changed, disease itself has not been eliminated. Sickness has been an integral part of the world of duality and the suffering that is the expectation of the ego-mind. Sickness will end when it no longer serves humanity—when sickness is not useful for your personal growth; when your fears are eliminated along with your beliefs and expectations relative to sickness; and when you and many others have succeeded in bringing the unlimited creative potential of your inner being into your physical experience.

The time has arrived when sickness and suffering are no longer needed by humanity for its personal growth. Beliefs that help maintain sickness are shifting, although they have not yet come to a place where a significant difference can be noted. We say again, *you do not* consciously *create disease in your body.* You are swimming in a sea of fear-driven messages, and beliefs about sickness and disease become sublimated in your conscious and unconscious belief systems. A deep fear of death, aging, and the process of dying can also take its toll on the individual and keep his or her focus on illness rather than optimum health.

The beliefs regarding sickness and aging are seen as truths because the beliefs themselves are so pervasive in your world. The beliefs, in turn, create the expected outcomes that, once again, confirm the beliefs. The relatively few examples to the contrary are not sufficient to change the broader view of society. When the Christ and his disciples healed the sick, they were able to do so because the one who was sick believed strongly enough that he or she would be cured. The belief that people have in their physicians has a similar effect—in fact this is an example of what is known as the "placebo effect." This ability to heal is within each of you and will be more easily harnessed when examples of these "miraculous" cures happen more often and are more visible. When this occurs, sickness and aging will diminish significantly. Death, on the other hand, will always exist. Death is the means by which you leave the physical plane of this life and transition back to your spiritual form. At the same time, death and the process of dying need not be painful or lingering. Death can be as simple as consciously lying down and releasing your spirit from the body. This will become more common when the fear of death and belief in suffering has been released.

The Body—Your Personal Canary

In this world of duality, your inner being has also used the body as a means of furthering spiritual growth. Dis-ease is highly descriptive, for a diseased body is one that is out of balance. The body's *natural* regenerative and recuperative properties are unable to carry out their innate function.

What causes this in the first place? You might use the analogy of the "canary in the coal mine." Miners used to carry a canary with them down into the depths of the mine. If the canary collapsed, this was an early indication that the air was bad and the miners should make a quick exit in order to avoid a similar fate. The physical body is like your personal canary. Your body will tell you if you are out of balance *relative to your thoughts and beliefs*, your work or pursuit of your life goals, your relationships and treatment of self or others, your addictions, and even your relationship to your environment. The body will "sing" out its warning to exit the cave when you are not fulfilling your inheritance upon this Earth. The body sings its song using pain and dis-ease. There may be other ways your inner being tries to get your attention, such as through a loss of a job or other difficulties. Nonetheless, the body will play the longest and loudest song until there is no more air and the life force is gone.

Your inner being's intention is for you to awaken to your spiritual nature and live in this wondrous physical environment in a state of joy, deep appreciation, and love for All. When you are in this place of unconditional love, your body reflects this. As noted previously, exceptions to this rule relate to souls who have come for a specific experience or challenge and/or out of their commitment to help certain other souls in their experience.

For most of you, the state of your body is a reflection of your state of mind and your approach to life. Beliefs and their closely related thoughts, words, and feelings, directly affect the well-being of the body. These, in turn, affect your energy signature. Worry, resentment, anger, negativity, feelings of unworthiness and other similar emotions have a cumulative affect on the body. Like Oscar Wilde's story of Dorian Gray, whose portrait became an ugly reflection of the state of his life, over time the body is affected by your own emotional well-being. Living your life in wonder and gratitude of the present moment, with a more complete understanding of your eternal and unlimited nature, and operating from your peaceful center, will greatly slow down the deterioration and aging of the body.

Learning to Listen to Your Body

Again, remember you have an unerring guidance system to tell you when you are out of harmony with your inner being and are, therefore, in a lower state of vibration. When a thought, belief, emotion, or action feels bad, you can actually experience the draining of energy from your body. The resulting vibration affects you at the cellular level. Eventually, dis-ease is the result. This is one reason laughter has been shown to be so healing. A man named Norman Cousins, when told he had a debilitating illness, greatly ameliorated this disease through watching and laughing at many comedic entertainment shows. He both changed his focus from his illness and raised his vibration through the joy of laughter, bringing his body back into harmony. The same can be said of those people who reduce their high blood pressure by petting their dog or cat. This pleasure is a form of love and has a high vibration and healing effect.

The Body as Beloved

Throughout this book, we have given you many ways in which you can consciously raise your vibration or energy signature and release the hold that the fear-based ego-mind has on your being. Look for ways throughout your day that you can nurture yourself and your body by accessing these tools. Over time, these tools become second nature and you more naturally reside in your peaceful center. You will be as the stillness below the water that is unaffected by the storms that trouble the water above.

No matter the current state of your body, treat the body as "the beloved." Your body has been your primary vehicle for experiencing and learning from this unique physical world. Love your body as it is right now and send it your appreciation. Like the plant that grows when you take care of its physical needs and flourishes when you speak lovingly to it, the body will react in a similar fashion. In Dr. Bruce Lipton's book, *The Biology of Belief,* he revealed through the scientific method how every cell in your body has consciousness and reacts to your thoughts and words. At the very least, stop talking negatively about your body. Cease your criticisms of its bulk, illnesses, features, or functions. Instead, flood your body with love and appreciation.

When you are walking, converse with your body. Admire how easily it moves, the strength of your muscles, the beating of your heart, the filling of your lungs, and the support of your bones and ligaments. When you work in the garden or paint that picture, send gratitude to your arms and hands that move at an unconscious level to your precise commands. Appreciate how you see through your eyes and how they help direct your movements. When you sit on the porch at the end of the day, thank your ears for bringing the music of the wind and the birds into your soul. Love your body even when the body appears to fail you, for this is the precious vehicle you chose to experience your life—to help you awaken to the larger and more glorious being that resides within you.

Use your beloved body to relish your wondrous physical world and to open you, through this experience, to the potential and joyful nature of your inner being. State your intention now . . . *"I love and deeply appreciate my beloved body. Every day I will speak lovingly of its many amazing features. Each night before I sleep I will bless and encourage every cell in my body to reach its highest state of well-being. I will use all the senses in my body to experience life and attend to what I am doing in the now. I will become an active partner with my body as we experience, with joy, our oneness with all of life."*

Chapter 9

Next Steps in Evolution

The evolutionary potential that resides within mankind can be fully realized through you. As this potential grows, a new type of society will arise out of this expanding number of enlightened beings. It is worthwhile for you to work toward your own inner peace. By doing so, you also help accelerate this evolution in humanity.

In this last chapter, we show how the creative process can be used to promote the expression of love on a steady, consistent basis. You will see how the potential of this world evolves as love becomes the more dominant mode of creation. Finally, we show that you are not alone in this evolutionary process, for the assistance of those in spirit is always available.

Positive Trends Upon Which to Focus

As compassionate individuals viewing your world, it is easy for each of you to become discouraged. You routinely observe the results of the fear-based ego-mind through the evidence of corporate greed, the abuse of power, despotism, bigotry, the suppression of individual freedom, cruelty of all kinds, and the destruction of your beautiful planet. While all of this exists, it is important to recognize the many positive signs, such as greater equality for women and people of color; the rising up of populations against oppressive leaders; a greater empathy with animals leading to positive changes in their treatment; a move toward organic, sustainable agriculture; and a heightened awareness of the part individuals can play in supporting the environment.

By historical standards, these changes are rapid. Furthermore, the rate of change is accelerating. You are a part of this change as you begin to disengage from the habits of your ego-mind while expressing the love of your inner being.

Using the Creative Process to Bring Forth Your Inner Being

A primary emphasis in this book has been to reassure you that you are the creator of your experience and your broader world. Although your current situation and the world at large may not be as you would like it, it should be encouraging to understand that you can use the creative process to change your tomorrow. Further, you can use the creative process to more directly bring forth your inner being. As a reminder, you use the creative process by:

Establishing Intention: Like the dedicated athlete or musician, keep in the forefront of your mind your deepest desire by holding an intention. You might write your intention down, referring to it daily. Perhaps your intention would read like this: *"It is my deepest intention to completely release the fear of my ego-mind while living in my natural state of being which is love. I am now open to this occurring at any time and in any way for my highest good."* Referring to this intention often will help shape your days until your actions more consistently align with your desire.

Becoming Aware of Your Thoughts and Words: You understand the power of your thoughts and words as they pertain to your energy signature as well as the creation of your experience. Since your words reflect the level at which you are vibrating, be compassionate with yourself and others, knowing that this core change takes effort. When you forget, you will notice your guidance system telling you your vibration is lower because of your thoughts, emotions, or words. This, then, is a good time to simply observe, breathe deeply, and release any attachment you have to judge yourself or others. Then make an effort to do better next time, until your words and thoughts are more reflective of your loving intention.

Examining and Realigning Your Beliefs: As we have said, time spent examining and changing the beliefs that are of low vibration or not in alignment with your unlimited spiritual nature is time well spent. Like the onion, start with the outside or with the most obvious beliefs that are troubling you. As you release these beliefs, other beliefs will come to the surface for your examination. When you eventually reach the core of your beliefs, change them to reflect your loving inner nature. For example, your new beliefs could read like this: *"I am a being of love. I am love incarnate. I am a part of all other beings who are also love incarnate."* These beliefs will resonate at a very high frequency, bringing you feelings of peace and joy.

Raising Your Vibration: Use your unerring guidance system to raise your vibration, knowing that this will bring you closer to your loving nature. When you realize you are out of sorts, use this guidance system as an opportunity to transform to a higher vibration or energy signature. Use all the tools in your toolbox in addition to those in your environment to assist you in gently returning to your peaceful center.

These four components of the creative process, if used regularly, will become second nature. Your inner guidance system tells you when you are out of sync with your loving inner being. Understand that this is a nudge from your inner being to evaluate your beliefs, words, or thoughts in order to understand how you might be sabotaging the life you would rather have. With consistent effort, your experience will become significantly more pleasant.

Don't Be Fooled by the Ego-Mind

We know that all of these activities are viewed as hard work. And, although change is the one constant in the universe, the ego-mind will resist change. The ego-mind is also very clever. It can take over your spiritual efforts by pointing out your "unworthiness," telling you that "you are not doing enough" or that "you are not changing fast enough" or "you are better than or not as good as others." Again, if your guidance system takes a nosedive, you know that these thoughts are not from your inner being. Your inner being, while providing gentle or not so gentle nudges, knows you are always in the perfect place for you. Your inner being also knows that the ultimate result of merging with your inner being cannot be stopped, for your inner being is who you are in truth.

We, therefore, urge you not to take yourself or life so seriously. As they say, *"lighten up"* or "en-*joy* the ride!" When you do so, you naturally raise your vibration, thus bringing yourself closer to your inner being.

The Ultimate Potential of Mankind

You are re-membering with your inner being and others are doing the same. It doesn't take a great deal of imagination to project how different the world will be when most beings operate from the basis of love rather than fear. Without judgment or condemnation, there will be peace among races, religions, and countries. Without the need to control or dominate each other, women, children, native populations, and even animals will be treated with respect. Without righteous retribution, people with addictions or who have broken the law will be provided with healing rather than punishment. Without greed, all beings will be provided the basic necessities of life. Further, your Mother Earth will be protected, nurtured, and respected. Each of you longs for these things. Yet the ego-mind is like the whirlwind that pulls you into indignation and horror by focusing on the negative rather than the positive aspects of humanity.

When you find yourself drawn into these negative perspectives, remind yourself that all that is not love is only the illusion you created to experience that which you are not. Since this illusion is something you no longer need for your spiritual growth, place your attention on the changes in society that reflect love rather than fear. You will then help these changes expand.

When you bring more of your spiritual nature into this physical world, your world will change. Even more fascinating will be the change in the creative potential within individuals. If you look toward the masters of love, such as Jesus Christ, the gurus and saints, you will see the potential that lies within all mankind—the ability to heal, bi-locate, live without food, manifest food, walk on water, depart the physical body at a predetermined time, part the seas, or even calm the weather. These masters did not do these things through ego-mind manipulation. Rather, they accomplished these feats through their open alignment with Source and their firm belief in their ability to create in this manner.

The most important outcome of your shift toward a more loving being will be the enjoyable feelings of peace and oneness with all of life. However, these "bells and whistles" or seemingly miraculous feats will be a natural extension of your loving inner being as "the spirit is made flesh."

Take Heart: All is Well

This world of planet Earth has been one of the most challenging of experiences. Only the most adventuresome of souls have relished this environment. This world has, in fact, taken you so far from the reality of your being that your awakening will provide you with a deeper understanding of who you really are. And, we beings that have never experienced this contrast will also, through our ties with you, gain a greater understanding of our own loving nature.

Knowing we are beings of love while experiencing only that fills us with joy. At the same time, without experiencing the opposite (powerlessness, fear, separation) our understanding is more limited. We have not watched you in judgment—we have watched you in awe and deep appreciation for this gift of understanding that you have given to the whole. You are deeply loved. You are also very much admired. We, therefore, experience much joy as we assist you in awakening to your loving inner being and to the understanding of how each of you is a great gift to the One.

Connecting with your inner being will be as if each of you are awakening from a dream. Your perception will be transformed. Your past difficulties will give you a tremendous appreciation and new way of viewing or experiencing this wondrous state of love. This is your reward for all the suffering—that, as well as the sheer exhilaration and sense of adventure that these diverse, albeit illusionary, experiences have provided. And, what an extraordinary adventure it has been! Think of your history, great books of literature, and movies. You have had villains along with heroes and each of you has played every part of the spectrum.

You will awaken to a new appreciation of this imaginative game of contrasts that you took part in creating. You will also relish the challenge as well as the joy in restoring your beautiful Gaia to her glory. Now you will undertake new adventures where love rather than fear dominates. All those in spirit are pleased with your progress and look forward to your creation of a new world order.

This New World is a Perception Away

To be an expression of love is goal number one—to bring your inner being into your daily life until the shift becomes permanent. Your guides, angels, and all other high spirit beings upon whom you can call stand ready to assist you in this transformation. Your strong intent, along with a continuous monitoring of your thoughts, words, and beliefs, will help bring this about. Your spiritual helpers on the other side will be working to raise the vibration of the planet so that your desire for a more benevolent world will come about.

You are not alone in this. You never have been. Call on us and we will respond. Once the shift has been made in your being, you will be ready to take the next step in working with others to create new societies and institutions based in love. You will have the ability to heal that which has been damaged; to bring about the beauty and vibration of spirit into the physical world.

The transformation of your world will have its bumps, for there will be great resistance from many still immersed in fear and separation. Your role will be to "judge not" as well as "resist not." Observe what is before you, turning your thoughts to a new vision. Place your attention on that which you wish to create. Know that all that is not love is an illusion, an illusion that is fading due to your intent and the intent of many others. In your view, the time for this transformation may seem long, yet in the annals of time, transformation will happen very quickly.

Do not let yourself be discouraged. Keep working on your own transformation from a being directed by the fear-driven ego-mind to a being who expresses his or her loving nature. Know that, more than anything else you can do, this will help bring about an end to the illusion of suffering. Anticipate what a proud and extraordinary moment that will be! In the meantime, go forth in joy. Look with wonder at the contrast and the illusion of the world. At the same time, see the love that lies beneath it. Remember you are a magnificent spiritual being—on that which you choose to focus, you will create. Direct yourself to the aspects of love—compassion, understanding, freedom, joy, peace, kindness, beauty, tenderness—and your creations will reflect this benevolence, magnifying to change your world. And so it is!

Creating the World of Our Dreams: A Meditation

We close with a meditation that will direct your creative energies, as well as that of others, toward a better world. May you watch with wonder the changes you are helping to create.

Step 1: Setting the Stage

Go to a quiet place where you will not be disturbed for five or ten minutes. You may wish to have soothing music playing in the background.

Step 2: Imagining

- *Use your imagination to experience living in the world of your dreams—a world of great beauty; where peace reigns; where all beings live in freedom, have their basic needs met, and give freely of their gifts. Imagine a world where the animals, fish, oceans, and the land are cherished; where people live long, healthy, vibrant, and fulfilling lives; where there is music, a joyful sense of community, and where love is the dominant mode of creation.*

- *Imagine all institutions, governments, and businesses operating from the fullness of love.*

- *See the oceans, rivers, streams, forests, land, and air purified and healed.*

- *Know that you are a powerful creator. You, along with many others, will make this dream a reality.*

Live the Dream

Awaken, go forth in joy and wonder, living the dream you wish to create!

Author's Note to the Reader

As with any channeled work, I have done my best to reflect the ideas of my higher guides, the Pegasus Group. However, their words inevitably flow through the filter of my experience. I, therefore, ask that you use your own inner wisdom as you read this book or any other. If the words or concepts resonate with your heart and discerning mind, feel free to make use of them. If the concepts are uncomfortable or do not resonate with your inner wisdom, simply put them aside.

Let love and your innate wisdom be your guide.